OECD/G20 Base Erosion and Profit Shifting Project

Country-by-Country Reporting – Compilation of 2022 Peer Review Reports

INCLUSIVE FRAMEWORK ON BEPS: ACTION 13

OECD
BETTER POLICIES FOR BETTER LIVES

Please cite this publication as:
OECD (2022), *Country-by-Country Reporting – Compilation of 2022 Peer Review Reports: Inclusive Framework on BEPS: Action 13*, OECD/G20 Base Erosion and Profit Shifting Project, OECD Publishing, Paris, https://doi.org/10.1787/5ea2ba65-en.

ISBN 978-92-64-89213-2 (print)
ISBN 978-92-64-83272-5 (pdf)
ISBN 978-92-64-43105-8 (HTML)
ISBN 978-92-64-75929-9 (epub)

OECD/G20 Base Erosion and Profit Shifting Project
ISSN 2313-2604 (print)
ISSN 2313-2612 (online)

Photo credits: Cover © ninog-Fotolia.com.

Corrigenda to publications may be found on line at: www.oecd.org/about/publishing/corrigenda.htm.

Foreword

Digitalisation and globalisation have had a profound impact on economies and the lives of people around the world, and this impact has only accelerated in the 21st century. These changes have brought with them challenges to the rules for taxing international business income, which have prevailed for more than a hundred years and created opportunities for base erosion and profit shifting (BEPS), requiring bold moves by policy makers to restore confidence in the system and ensure that profits are taxed where economic activities take place and value is created.

In 2013, the OECD ramped up efforts to address these challenges in response to growing public and political concerns about tax avoidance by large multinationals. The OECD and G20 countries joined forces and developed an Action Plan to address BEPS in September 2013. The Action Plan identified 15 actions aimed at introducing coherence in the domestic rules that affect cross-border activities, reinforcing substance requirements in the existing international standards, and improving transparency as well as certainty.

After two years of work, measures in response to the 15 actions, including those published in an interim form in 2014, were consolidated into a comprehensive package and delivered to G20 Leaders in November 2015. The BEPS package represents the first substantial renovation of the international tax rules in almost a century. As the BEPS measures are implemented, it is expected that profits will be reported where the economic activities that generate them are carried out and where value is created. BEPS planning strategies that rely on outdated rules or on poorly co-ordinated domestic measures will be rendered ineffective.

OECD and G20 countries also agreed to continue to work together to ensure a consistent and co ordinated implementation of the BEPS recommendations and to make the project more inclusive. As a result, they created the OECD/G20 Inclusive Framework on BEPS (Inclusive Framework), bringing all interested and committed countries and jurisdictions on an equal footing in the Committee on Fiscal Affairs and its subsidiary bodies. With over 140 members, the Inclusive Framework monitors and peer reviews the implementation of the minimum standards and is completing the work on standard setting to address BEPS issues. In addition to its members, other international organisations and regional tax bodies are involved in the work of the Inclusive Framework, which also consults business and the civil society on its different work streams.

Although implementation of the BEPS package is dramatically changing the international tax landscape and improving the fairness of tax systems, one of the key outstanding BEPS issues – to address the tax challenges arising from the digitalisation of the economy – remained unresolved. In a major step forward on 8 October 2021, over 135 Inclusive Framework members, representing more than 95% of global GDP, joined a two-pillar solution to reform the international taxation rules and ensure that multinational enterprises pay a fair share of tax wherever they operate and generate profits in today's digitalised and globalised world economy. The implementation of these new rules is envisaged by 2023.

This report was approved by the Inclusive Framework on 13 September 2022 and prepared for publication by the OECD Secretariat.

Table of contents

Abbreviations and acronyms

AEOI	Automatic Exchange of Information
BEPS	Base Erosion and Profit Shifting
CAA	Competent Authority Agreement
CbC	Country-by-Country
CbCR	Country-by-Country Reporting
CTS	Common Transmission System
DTC	Double Tax Convention
EOI	Exchange of Information
EU	European Union
MAAC	Convention on Mutual Administrative Assistance in Tax Matters
MCAA	Multilateral Competent Authority Agreement
MNE	Multinational Enterprise
OECD	Organisation for Economic Co-operation and Development
PE	Permanent Establishment
QCAA	Qualifying Competent Authority Agreement
SPE	Surrogate Parent Entity
TIEA	Tax Information Exchange Agreement
TP	Transfer Pricing
UPE	Ultimate Parent Entity
XML	Extensible Mark-up Language

Executive summary

Context of Country-by-Country Reporting

1. A key component of the transparency pillar of the OECD/G20 Base Erosion and Profit Shifting (BEPS) Project is the obligation for all large multinational enterprise groups (MNE Groups) with consolidated group revenue above an agreed threshold to file a Country-by-Country (CbC) report. The *Transfer Pricing Documentation and Country-by-Country Reporting, Action 13 - 2015 Final Report* provides a template for these MNE Groups to report annually, and for each tax jurisdiction in which they do business, the amount of revenue, profit before income tax and income tax paid and accrued, as well as the number of employees, stated capital, retained earnings and tangible assets. MNE Groups should also identify each entity within the group doing business in a particular jurisdiction and provide an indication of the business activities each entity is engaged in. As a result of BEPS Action 13, tax administrations around the world are receiving information on large foreign-headed MNE Groups which was not previously available, enabling them to better understand the structure of a group's business and enhancing their risk assessment capacity.

2. In general, the Ultimate Parent Entity (UPE) of an MNE Group will prepare and file its CbC report with the tax administration in its jurisdiction of tax residence. That tax administration will automatically exchange the CbC report with the tax administration in each jurisdiction listed in the CbC report as being a place in which the MNE Group has a Constituent Entity resident for tax purposes. This will be carried out under an International Agreement (such as the Multilateral Convention on Mutual Administrative Assistance in Tax Matters (MAAC), a Double Tax Convention (DTC) or a Tax Information Exchange Agreement (TIEA) permitting automatic exchange of information (AEOI). A Qualifying Competent Authority Agreement (QCAA) that sets out the operational details of the exchange of CbC reports will also need to be in place.

3. As one of the four BEPS minimum standards, the Country-by-Country reporting (CbCR) requirements contained in *Transfer Pricing Documentation and Country-by-Country Reporting, Action 13 - 2015 Final Report* are subject to peer review in order to ensure timely and accurate implementation and thus safeguard the level playing field. All members of the Inclusive Framework on BEPS (the Inclusive Framework) commit to implementing the BEPS Action 13 minimum standard and to participating in the peer review, on an equal footing.

4. Implementation of CbC reporting is well advanced as the peer review process evidences, with over 100 jurisdictions having now introduced an obligation for relevant MNE Groups to file a CbC report in their domestic legal framework.

Scope of this review

5. This is the fifth annual peer review for the BEPS Action 13 minimum standard. It covers 134 jurisdictions which provided legislation and/or information relating to their implementation of CbC Reporting.[1]

6. For each jurisdiction, the review covers the domestic legal and administrative framework, the exchange of information framework and measures in place to ensure the confidentiality and appropriate use of CbC reports.

Key findings

7. The key findings of the fifth annual peer review are as follows:

- ***Domestic legal and administrative framework***: Over 100 jurisdictions have a domestic legal framework for CbC reporting in place. In addition, a number of jurisdictions have final legislation approved that is awaiting official publication. In this peer review report, 28 jurisdictions have received a general recommendation to put in place or finalise their domestic legal or administrative framework and 27 jurisdictions received one or more recommendations for improvements to specific areas of their framework. Furthermore, two jurisdictions finalised legislation during this peer review period but it has not been possible to carry out a review of that legislation. A review of the legislation will take place in the next peer review.
- **Exchange of information framework**: Of the jurisdictions included in this review, 82 jurisdictions have multilateral or bilateral competent authority agreements in place.
- **Confidentiality**: Of the jurisdictions included in this review, 88 have undergone an assessment by the Global Forum on Transparency and Exchange of Information for Tax Purposes (the Global Forum) concerning confidentiality and data safeguards in the context of implementing the AEOI standard, and did not receive any action plan.
- **Appropriate use**: Of the jurisdictions included in this review, 64 jurisdictions have provided detailed information, enabling the Inclusive Framework to obtain sufficient assurance that measures are in place to ensure the appropriate use of CbC reports.

8. During the course of this peer review, a number of jurisdictions reported delays in the implementation of CbC reporting, or in the filing and exchange of CbC reports, resulting from the impact of the COVID-19 pandemic. As these concern issues beyond the control of tax administrations, and there is no reason to believe they will persist once the pandemic comes to an end, these delays are not highlighted in each jurisdiction's peer review and no recommendation is made. If delays continue into periods covered by future peer reviews, they will be considered in the context of the global situation at that time.

9. A number of Inclusive Framework members are not included in this peer review report, either because they joined the Inclusive Framework after 1 October 2021 (at which point it was too late to incorporate them into the current peer review process) or they opted out of the peer review in accordance with the peer review terms of reference. Jurisdictions opting out of the peer review are required to confirm that they do not have any resident entities that are the UPE of an MNE Group above the consolidated group revenue threshold and that they will not require local filing of CbC reports. Members of the Inclusive Framework that are not included in this peer review report are:

- Albania
- Burkina Faso
- Cook Islands
- Mauritania
- Saint Kitts and Nevis
- Samoa

Next steps

10. The peer review of the BEPS Action 13 minimum standard is an annual process. Work will continue to monitor the implementation and operation of CbC reporting by members of the Inclusive Framework and to highlight progress made by jurisdictions to address recommendations that have been made.

Note

[1] The Russian Federation has not been included in the peer review process for this year. A copy of the Russian Federation's peer review report for 2021 is included in this report for information.

1 The peer review of the BEPS Action 13 minimum standard on Country-by-Country Reporting

Background

11. The Country-by-Country (CbC) reporting requirements contained in the 2015 BEPS Action 13 Report (OECD, 2015[1]) form one of the four BEPS minimum standards. Each of the four BEPS minimum standards is subject to peer review in order to ensure timely and accurate implementation and thus safeguard the level playing field. All members of the Inclusive Framework commit to implementing the BEPS Action 13 minimum standard and to participating in the peer review, on an equal footing.

12. The purpose of a peer review is to ensure the effective and consistent implementation of an agreed standard and to recognise progress made by jurisdictions in this regard.

13. The peer review is a review of the legal and administrative framework put in place by a jurisdiction to implement the CbC reporting standard.

Outline of the key aspects assessed in the annual report

14. This peer review report contains the findings of the fifth annual peer review process undertaken by an Ad Hoc Joint Working Party 6 / Working Party 10 sub-group referred to as the "CbC Reporting Group". This focuses on each jurisdiction's domestic legal and administrative framework, its exchange of information network, and its measures to ensure the confidentiality and appropriate use of CbC reports.

15. The structure of each section relating to a specific reviewed jurisdiction is as follows:

- summary of filing requirements
- a table summarising any recommendations issued
- domestic legal and administrative framework
- exchange of information
- appropriate use.

16. Jurisdictions which joined the Inclusive Framework after 1 October 2021 have not been reviewed as part of this annual peer review process. These jurisdictions will be included in the next peer review process.

17. This peer review evaluates an Inclusive Framework member's implementation of the BEPS Action 13 minimum standard against an agreed set of criteria.[1] These criteria are set out in terms of reference, which include each of the elements that a jurisdiction needs to demonstrate it has fulfilled in order to show proper implementation of the standard. These terms of reference are supplemented by additional questions

for jurisdictions concerning measures they have implemented to ensure the appropriate use of CbC reporting information.

18. An agreed peer review methodology sets out the process for undertaking peer reviews of jurisdictions' compliance with the BEPS Action 13 minimum standard on Country-by-Country (CbC) reporting. This methodology sets out the scope of the peer review, the information that will be used to conduct reviews, the timelines and procedures for a review, an outline of a peer review report, the process for discussion and approval of reviews, and the confidentiality of peer review documents. A new methodology published in 2020 replaces one agreed by the Inclusive Framework in 2017, which expired with the completion of the third annual peer review in September 2020. There has been no change to the terms of reference agreed by the Inclusive Framework in 2017.

19. The Global Forum has conducted preliminary expert assessments of confidentiality and data safeguards with respect to the standard on automatic exchange of information. Given its expertise in this area, the CbC Reporting Group has relied on the work and conclusions of the Global Forum. As it contains non-public information on jurisdictions' internal systems and procedures, the outcomes of that work are not published and no further details of the review of confidentiality are provided in this compilation of peer review reports.

20. The terms of reference and methodology do not alter the BEPS Action 13 minimum standard. Any terms used in the terms of reference or methodology, and capitalised terms in this report, take their meaning from the language and context of the 2015 BEPS Action 13 Report and the references therein.

21. Jurisdictions' individual sections in this report generally reflect the status of implementation as of 31 March 2022 with the exception of information on the exchange of CbC reports which reflects the position as of 31 December 2021.

References

OECD (2020), *BEPS Action 13 on Country-by-Country Reporting – Peer Review Documents: October 2020*, OECD/G20 Base Erosion and Profit Shifting Project, OECD, https://www.oecd.org/tax/beps/beps-action-13-on-country-by-country-reporting-peer-review-documents.pdf. [2]

OECD (2015), *Transfer Pricing Documentation and Country-by-Country Reporting, Action 13 - 2015 Final Report*, OECD/G20 Base Erosion and Profit Shifting Project, OECD Publishing, Paris, https://doi.org/10.1787/9789264241480-en. [1]

Note

[1] https://www.oecd.org/tax/beps/beps-action-13-on-country-by-country-reporting-peer-review-documents.pdf (approved by the Inclusive Framework in October 2020 (OECD, 2020[2])).

2 Peer review reports

Andorra

Overview of CbC reporting requirements

First reporting fiscal year: Commencing on or after 1 January 2018

Consolidated group revenue threshold: EUR 750 million

Filing deadline: 12 months following the end of the reporting fiscal year

Local filing required: Yes

Surrogate parent entity filing permitted: Yes

First review of the domestic legal framework: 2017/2018

Summary of recommendations

Area of implementation	Recommendations for improvement
Domestic legal and administrative framework	None.
Exchange of information framework	None.
Appropriate use	None.

The domestic legal and administrative framework

Andorra confirms that its rules have not changed and continue to be applied effectively. Andorra continues to meet all terms of reference.

The exchange of information framework

Andorra's 2018/2019 peer review contained a recommendation that Andorra take steps to implement processes or written procedures to ensure that the exchange of information is conducted in a manner consistent with the terms of reference relating to the exchange of information framework ahead of its first exchanges of information. Further information has been received showing that these processes are in place and this recommendation is now removed.

Appropriate use of CbC reports

Andorra confirms that its rules have not changed and continue to be applied effectively. Andorra continues to meet all terms of reference.

Angola

Overview of CbC reporting requirements

Angola has not yet introduced a requirement for the filing of CbC reports, as required under the BEPS Action 13 (CbC reporting) minimum standard.

Summary of recommendations

Area of implementation	Recommendations for improvement
Domestic legal and administrative framework	It is recommended that Angola take steps to implement a domestic legal and administrative framework to impose and enforce CbC reporting requirements as soon as possible.
Exchange of information framework	It is recommended that Angola take steps to have qualifying competent authority agreements in effect with jurisdictions of the Inclusive Framework that meet the confidentiality, consistency and appropriate use conditions and with which Angola has an international exchange of information agreement in effect that allows for the automatic exchange of tax information. It is recommended that Angola take steps to implement the necessary processes or written procedures to ensure that the exchange of information is conducted in a manner consistent with the terms of reference relating to the exchange of information framework.
Appropriate use	It is recommended that Angola take steps to ensure that the appropriate use condition is met ahead of the first exchanges of information.

The domestic legal and administrative framework

Angola does not yet have legislation in place to implement the BEPS Action 13 minimum standard.

It is recommended that Angola take steps to implement a domestic legal and administrative framework to impose and enforce CbC reporting requirements as soon as possible. This recommendation remains in place since the 2017/2018 peer review.

The exchange of information framework

Angola has no bilateral relationships in place for the exchange of CbC reports nor processes to ensure that the exchange of information is conducted in a manner consistent with the terms of reference relating to the exchange of information framework.

It is recommended that Angola take steps to have qualifying competent authority agreements in effect with jurisdictions of the Inclusive Framework that meet the confidentiality, consistency and appropriate use conditions and with which Angola has an international exchange of information agreement in effect that allows for the automatic exchange of tax information. This recommendation remains in place since the 2017/2018 peer review.

It is recommended that Angola take steps to implement the necessary processes or written procedures to ensure that the exchange of information is conducted in a manner consistent with the terms of reference relating to the exchange of information framework. This recommendation remains in place since the 2018/2019 peer review.

Appropriate use of CbC reports

Angola does not yet have controls in place to ensure the appropriate use of CbC reports.

It is recommended that Angola take steps to ensure that the appropriate use condition is met ahead of the first exchanges of information. This recommendation remains in place since the 2017/2018 peer review.

Anguilla

Overview of CbC reporting requirements

First reporting fiscal year: Commencing on or after 1 January 2019

Consolidated group revenue threshold: USD 850 million

Filing deadline: 12 months following the end of the reporting fiscal year

Local filing required: No

Surrogate parent entity filing permitted: Yes

First review of the domestic legal framework: 2018/2019

Summary of recommendations

Area of implementation	Recommendations for improvement
Domestic legal and administrative framework	None.
Exchange of information framework	None.
Appropriate use	Not reviewed.

The domestic legal and administrative framework

Anguilla confirms that its rules have not changed and continue to be applied effectively. Anguilla continues to meet all terms of reference.

The exchange of information framework

Anguilla's 2020/2021 peer review included a recommendation that Anguilla have systems in place to ensure all expected reports are received and all exchanges are completed and recorded in a timely manner. Anguilla has provided the required information on reports received and exchanged to evidence that, and that recommendation is removed.

Appropriate use of CbC reports

Anguilla is a non-reciprocal jurisdiction and, as such, will not receive CbC reports submitted to tax authorities in other jurisdictions, and will not apply local filing. It is therefore not necessary for this peer review evaluation to reach any conclusions with respect to Anguilla's compliance with the terms of reference on appropriate use.

Antigua and Barbuda

Overview of CbC reporting requirements

Antigua and Barbuda has not yet introduced a requirement for the filing of CbC reports, as required under the BEPS Action 13 (CbC reporting) minimum standard.

Summary of recommendations

Area of implementation	Recommendations for improvement
Domestic legal and administrative framework	It is recommended that Antigua and Barbuda take steps to implement a domestic legal and administrative framework to impose and enforce CbC reporting requirements as soon as possible.
Exchange of information framework	It is recommended that Antigua and Barbuda take steps to have qualifying competent authority agreements in effect with jurisdictions of the Inclusive Framework that meet the confidentiality, consistency and appropriate use conditions and with which Antigua and Barbuda has an international exchange of information agreement in effect that allows for the automatic exchange of tax information. It is recommended that Antigua and Barbuda take steps to implement the necessary processes or written procedures to ensure that the exchange of information is conducted in a manner consistent with the terms of reference relating to the exchange of information framework.
Appropriate use	It is recommended that Antigua and Barbuda take steps to ensure that the appropriate use condition is met ahead of the first exchanges of information.

The domestic legal and administrative framework

Antigua and Barbuda does not yet have legislation in place to implement the BEPS Action 13 minimum standard.

It is recommended that Antigua and Barbuda take steps to implement a domestic legal and administrative framework to impose and enforce CbC reporting requirements as soon as possible. This recommendation remains in place since the 2019/2020 peer review.

The exchange of information framework

Antigua and Barbuda has no bilateral relationships in place for the exchange of CbC reports nor processes to ensure that the exchange of information is conducted in a manner consistent with the terms of reference relating to the exchange of information framework.

It is recommended that Antigua and Barbuda take steps to have qualifying competent authority agreements in effect with jurisdictions of the Inclusive Framework that meet the confidentiality, consistency and appropriate use conditions and with which Antigua and Barbuda has an international exchange of information agreement in effect that allows for the automatic exchange of tax information. This recommendation remains in place since the 2019/2020 peer review.

It is recommended that Antigua and Barbuda take steps to implement the necessary processes or written procedures to ensure that the exchange of information is conducted in a manner consistent with the terms of reference relating to the exchange of information framework. This recommendation remains in place since the 2019/2020 peer review.

Appropriate use of CbC reports

Antigua and Barbuda does not yet have controls in place to ensure the appropriate use of CbC reports.

It is recommended that Antigua and Barbuda take steps to ensure that the appropriate use condition is met ahead of the first exchanges of information. This recommendation remains in place since the 2019/2020 peer review.

Argentina

Overview of CbC reporting requirements

First reporting fiscal year: Commencing on or after 1 January 2017

Consolidated group revenue threshold: EUR 750 million

Filing deadline: 12 months following the end of the reporting fiscal year

Local filing required: Yes

Surrogate parent entity filing permitted: Yes

First review of the domestic legal framework: 2017/2018

Summary of recommendations

Area of implementation	Recommendations for improvement
Domestic legal and administrative framework	None.
Exchange of information framework	None.
Appropriate use	None.

The domestic legal and administrative framework

Argentina confirms that its rules have not changed and continue to be applied effectively. Argentina continues to meet all terms of reference.

The exchange of information framework

Argentina confirms that its rules have not changed and continue to be applied effectively. Argentina continues to meet all terms of reference.

Appropriate use of CbC reports

Argentina confirms that its rules have not changed and continue to be applied effectively. Argentina continues to meet all terms of reference.

Armenia

Overview of CbC reporting requirements

Armenia has not yet introduced a requirement for the filing of CbC reports, as required under the BEPS Action 13 (CbC reporting) minimum standard.

Summary of recommendations

Area of implementation	Recommendations for improvement
Domestic legal and administrative framework	It is recommended that Armenia take steps to implement a domestic legal and administrative framework to impose and enforce CbC reporting requirements as soon as possible.
Exchange of information framework	It is recommended that Armenia take steps to have qualifying competent authority agreements in effect with jurisdictions of the Inclusive Framework that meet the confidentiality, consistency and appropriate use conditions and with which Armenia has an international exchange of information agreement in effect that allows for the automatic exchange of tax information. It is recommended that Armenia take steps to implement the necessary processes or written procedures to ensure that the exchange of information is conducted in a manner consistent with the terms of reference relating to the exchange of information framework.
Appropriate use	It is recommended that Armenia take steps to ensure that the appropriate use condition is met ahead of the first exchanges of information.

The domestic legal and administrative framework

Armenia does not yet have legislation in place to implement the BEPS Action 13 minimum standard.

It is recommended that Armenia take steps to implement a domestic legal and administrative framework to impose and enforce CbC reporting requirements as soon as possible. This recommendation remains in place since the 2019/2020 peer review.

The exchange of information framework

Armenia has no bilateral relationships in place for the exchange of CbC reports nor processes to ensure that the exchange of information is conducted in a manner consistent with the terms of reference relating to the exchange of information framework.

It is recommended that Armenia take steps to have qualifying competent authority agreements in effect with jurisdictions of the Inclusive Framework that meet the confidentiality, consistency and appropriate use conditions and with which Armenia has an international exchange of information agreement in effect that allows for the automatic exchange of tax information. This recommendation remains in place since the 2019/2020 peer review.

It is recommended that Armenia take steps to implement the necessary processes or written procedures to ensure that the exchange of information is conducted in a manner consistent with the terms of reference relating to the exchange of information framework. This recommendation remains in place since the 2019/2020 peer review.

Appropriate use of CbC reports

Armenia does not yet have controls in place to ensure the appropriate use of CbC reports.

It is recommended that Armenia take steps to ensure that the appropriate use condition is met ahead of the first exchanges of information. This recommendation remains in place since the 2019/2020 peer review.

Aruba

Overview of CbC reporting requirements

First reporting fiscal year: Commencing on or after 1 January 2019

Consolidated group revenue threshold: AWG 1,500 million

Filing deadline: 12 months following the end of the reporting fiscal year

Local filing required: Requirement suspended

Surrogate parent entity filing permitted: Yes

First review of the domestic legal framework: 2020/2021

Summary of recommendations

Area of implementation	Recommendations for improvement
Domestic legal and administrative framework	It is recommended that Aruba clarify that the annual consolidated group revenue threshold calculation rule applies in line with the OECD guidance on currency fluctuations in respect of an MNE Group whose Ultimate Parent Entity is located in a jurisdiction other than Aruba.
Exchange of information framework	It is recommended that Aruba take steps to have qualifying competent authority agreements in effect with jurisdictions of the Inclusive Framework that meet the confidentiality, consistency and appropriate use conditions and with which Aruba has an international exchange of information agreement in effect that allows for the automatic exchange of tax information. It is recommended that Aruba take steps to implement the necessary processes or written procedures to ensure that the exchange of information is conducted in a manner consistent with the terms of reference relating to the exchange of information framework.
Appropriate use	It is recommended that Aruba take steps to ensure that the appropriate use condition is met ahead of the first exchanges of information.

The domestic legal and administrative framework

Aruba's 2020/2021 report included a recommendation that Aruba take steps to amend its legislation or otherwise clarify that local filing in Aruba is only required in line with the minimum standard for Action 13. Aruba has suspended local filing by issuing a statement and this recommendation is therefore removed.[1]

It is recommended that Aruba clarify that the annual consolidated group revenue threshold calculation rule applies in line with the OECD guidance on currency fluctuations in respect of an MNE Group whose Ultimate Parent Entity is located in a jurisdiction other than Aruba. This recommendation remains in place since the 2020/2021 peer review.

Aruba's domestic legal and administrative framework meets all other terms of reference.

The exchange of information framework

Aruba has no bilateral relationships in place for the exchange of CbC reports nor processes to ensure that the exchange of information is conducted in a manner consistent with the terms of reference relating to the exchange of information framework

It is recommended that Aruba take steps to have qualifying competent authority agreements in effect with jurisdictions of the Inclusive Framework that meet the confidentiality, consistency and appropriate use conditions and with which Aruba has an international exchange of information agreement in effect that allows for the automatic exchange of tax information. This recommendation remains in place since the 2018/2019 peer review.

It is recommended that Aruba take steps to implement the necessary processes or written procedures to ensure that the exchange of information is conducted in a manner consistent with the terms of reference relating to the exchange of information framework. This recommendation remains in place since the 2018/2019 peer review.

Appropriate use of CbC reports

Aruba does not yet have controls in place to ensure the appropriate use of CbC reports.

It is recommended that Aruba take steps to ensure that the appropriate use condition is met. This recommendation remains in place since the 2018/2019 peer review.

Note

[1] https://www.impuesto.aw/cbc.

Australia

Overview of CbC reporting requirements

First reporting fiscal year: Commencing on or after 1 January 2016

Consolidated group revenue threshold: AUD 1 billion

Filing deadline: 12 months following the end of the reporting fiscal year

Local filing required: Yes

Surrogate parent entity filing permitted: Yes

First review of the domestic legal framework: 2017/2018

Summary of recommendations

Area of implementation	Recommendations for improvement
Domestic legal and administrative framework	None.
Exchange of information framework	None.
Appropriate use	None.

The domestic legal and administrative framework

Australia confirms that its rules have not changed and continue to be applied effectively. Australia continues to meet all terms of reference.

The exchange of information framework

Australia made some exchanges of CbC reports after the deadline. This was caused by delay on a technical upgrade that has since been resolved and so no recommendation is required.

Australia confirms that its rules have not changed and continue to be applied effectively. Australia continues to meet all terms of reference.

Appropriate use of CbC reports

Australia confirms that its rules have not changed and continue to be applied effectively. Australia continues to meet all terms of reference.

Austria

Overview of CbC reporting requirements

First reporting fiscal year: Commencing on or after 1 January 2016

Consolidated group revenue threshold: EUR 750 million

Filing deadline: 12 months following the end of the reporting fiscal year

Local filing required: Yes, for reporting fiscal years commencing on or after 1 January 2017

Surrogate parent entity filing permitted: Yes

First review of the domestic legal framework: 2017/2018

Summary of recommendations

Area of implementation	Recommendations for improvement
Domestic legal and administrative framework	None.
Exchange of information framework	None.
Appropriate use	None.

The domestic legal and administrative framework

Austria confirms that its rules have not changed and continue to be applied effectively. Austria continues to meet all terms of reference.

The exchange of information framework

Austria confirms that its rules have not changed and continue to be applied effectively. Austria continues to meet all terms of reference.

Appropriate use of CbC reports

Austria confirms that its rules have not changed and continue to be applied effectively. Austria continues to meet all terms of reference.

Bahamas

Overview of CbC reporting requirements

First reporting fiscal year: Commencing on or after 1 January 2018

Consolidated group revenue threshold: USD 850 million

Filing deadline: 12 months following the end of the reporting fiscal year

Local filing required: No

Surrogate parent entity filing permitted: Yes

First review of the domestic legal framework: 2018/2019

Summary of recommendations

Area of implementation	Recommendations for improvement
Domestic legal and administrative framework	None.
Exchange of information framework	None.
Appropriate use	None.

The domestic legal and administrative framework

The Bahamas confirms that its rules have not changed and continue to be applied effectively. The Bahamas continues to meet all terms of reference.[1]

The Bahamas' 2018/2019 peer review included a monitoring point relating to having no specific processes in place that would allow the Bahamas to take appropriate measures in case it is notified by another jurisdiction that such other jurisdiction has reason to believe that an error may have led to incorrect or incomplete information reporting by a Reporting Entity or that there is non-compliance of a Reporting Entity with respect to its obligation to file a CbC report. The Bahamas has provided information to demonstrate that such processes are now in place and as such this monitoring point is now removed.

The exchange of information framework

In its 2018/2019 peer report it was recommended that the Bahamas take steps to implement processes or written procedures to ensure that the exchange of information in conducted in a manner consistent with the terms of reference relating to the exchange of information framework ahead of its first exchanges of information. These processes are now in place and the recommendation is removed.

Appropriate use of CbC reports

The Bahamas confirms that its rules have not changed and continue to be applied effectively. The Bahamas continues to meet all terms of reference

Note

[1] The Bahamas' 2018/2019 peer review included a monitoring point which remains in place. It was noted that the Bahamas' legislation does not include a local filing provision but does include provisions relating to (i) the deactivation of local filing in case of surrogate filing (see Section 3(4) of The Bahamas CbC Act) and (ii) the fact that a single Constituent Entity could file a CbC report that satisfies the filing requirement of all Constituent Entities of such MNE Group that are resident in the Bahamas (see Section 3(3) of The Bahamas CbC Act). While these provisions do not seem to create a local filing obligation on Constituent Entities in the Bahamas (being noted that according to Section 3(1) and 3(2), only Ultimate Parent Entities and Surrogate Parent Entities shall file a CbC report in the Bahamas), they may introduce uncertainty for taxpayers. This will be monitored to ensure that no local filing obligations arise from Section 3 of the act.

Bahrain

Overview of CbC reporting requirements

First reporting fiscal year: Commencing on or after 1 January 2021

Consolidated group revenue threshold: BHD 342 million

Filing deadline: 12 months following the end of the reporting fiscal year

Local filing required: No

Surrogate parent entity filing permitted: No

First review of the domestic legal framework: 2020/2021

Summary of recommendations

Area of implementation	Recommendations for improvement
Domestic legal and administrative framework	None.
Exchange of information framework	None.
Appropriate use	Not reviewed.

The domestic legal and administrative framework

Bahrain confirms that its rules have not changed and continue to be applied effectively. Bahrain continues to meet all terms of reference.

The exchange of information framework

In its 2018/2019 peer review, it was recommended that Bahrain take steps to implement the necessary processes or written procedures to ensure that the exchange of information is conducted in a manner consistent with the terms of reference relating to the exchange of information framework. These processes are now in place and the recommendation is removed.

Appropriate use of CbC reports

Bahrain is a non-reciprocal jurisdiction and, as such, will not receive CbC reports submitted to tax authorities in other jurisdictions, and will not apply local filing. It is therefore not necessary for this peer review evaluation to reach any conclusions with respect to compliance with the terms of reference on appropriate use.

Barbados

Overview of CbC reporting requirements

First reporting fiscal year: Commencing on or after 1 January 2021

Consolidated group revenue threshold: USD 850 million

Filing deadline: 12 months following the end of the reporting fiscal year

Local filing required: Yes

Surrogate parent entity filing permitted: Yes

First review of the domestic legal framework: 2021/2022

Summary of recommendations

Area of implementation	Recommendations for improvement
Domestic legal and administrative framework	None.
Exchange of information framework	None.
Appropriate use	None.

The domestic legal and administrative framework

In the 2017/2018 peer review, it was recommended that Barbados take steps to implement a domestic legal and administrative framework to impose and enforce CbC reporting requirements as soon as possible. Barbados has now introduced a CbC reporting filing requirement which applies to all Ultimate Parent Entities of MNE Groups above a certain threshold and which requires inclusion of all constituent entities. This recommendation is therefore removed.[1]

A CbC reporting filing obligation applies in Barbados for fiscal years commencing on or after 1 January 2021 and filing is required 12 months after the reporting year end. Barbados has enforcement requirements to ensure compliance with rules on CbC reporting.

Barbados's domestic legal and administrative framework meets all the terms of reference.

The exchange of information framework

In the 2017/2018 peer review, it was recommended that Barbados take steps to have qualifying competent authority agreements in effect with jurisdictions of the Inclusive Framework that meet the confidentiality, consistency and appropriate use conditions and with which Barbados has an international exchange of information agreement in effect that allows for the automatic exchange of tax information. Barbados has activated relationships under the Multilateral Competent Authority Agreement for the exchange of CbC reports and this recommendation is removed.

In the 2018/2019 peer review, it was recommended that Barbados take steps to implement the necessary processes or written procedures to ensure that the exchange of information is conducted in a manner consistent with the terms of reference relating to the exchange of information framework. These processes are now in place and the recommendation is removed.

Appropriate use of CbC reports

In the 2017/2018 peer review, it was recommended that Barbados take steps to ensure that the appropriate use condition is met ahead of the first exchanges of information. Barbados now has controls in place to ensure the appropriate use of CbC reports and this recommendation is removed.

Note

[1] https://bra.gov.bb/Download.ashx?file=Attachments%2fIncome+tax+(Country+by+Country+reporting)+Act+2021-27.pdf&name=Income+Tax+(Country-by-Country+Reporting)+Act+2021-27.

Belarus

Overview of CbC reporting requirements

Belarus has not yet introduced a requirement for the filing of CbC reports, as required under the BEPS Action 13 (CbC reporting) minimum standard.

Summary of recommendations

Area of implementation	Recommendations for improvement
Domestic legal and administrative framework	It is recommended that Belarus take steps to implement a domestic legal and administrative framework to impose and enforce CbC reporting requirements as soon as possible.
Exchange of information framework	It is recommended that Belarus take steps to have qualifying competent authority agreements in effect with jurisdictions of the Inclusive Framework that meet the confidentiality, consistency and appropriate use conditions and with which Belarus has an international exchange of information agreement in effect that allows for the automatic exchange of tax information. It is recommended that Belarus take steps to implement the necessary processes or written procedures to ensure that the exchange of information is conducted in a manner consistent with the terms of reference relating to the exchange of information framework.
Appropriate use	It is recommended that Belarus take steps to ensure that the appropriate use condition is met ahead of the first exchanges of information.

The domestic legal and administrative framework

Belarus does not yet have legislation in place to implement the BEPS Action 13 minimum standard.

It is recommended that Belarus take steps to implement a domestic legal and administrative framework to impose and enforce CbC reporting requirements as soon as possible.

The exchange of information framework

Belarus has no bilateral relationships in place for the exchange of CbC reports nor processes to ensure that the exchange of information is conducted in a manner consistent with the terms of reference relating to the exchange of information framework.

It is recommended that Belarus take steps to have qualifying competent authority agreements in effect with jurisdictions of the Inclusive Framework that meet the confidentiality, consistency and appropriate use conditions and with which Belarus has an international exchange of information agreement in effect that allows for the automatic exchange of tax information.

It is recommended that Belarus take steps to implement the necessary processes or written procedures to ensure that the exchange of information is conducted in a manner consistent with the terms of reference relating to the exchange of information framework.

Appropriate use of CbC reports

Belarus does not yet have controls in place to ensure the appropriate use of CbC reports.

It is recommended that Belarus take steps to ensure that the appropriate use condition is met ahead of the first exchanges of information.

Belgium

Overview of CbC reporting requirements

First reporting fiscal year: Commencing on or after 1 January 2016

Consolidated group revenue threshold: EUR 750 million

Filing deadline: 12 months following the end of the reporting fiscal year

Local filing required: Yes

Surrogate parent entity filing permitted: Yes

First review of the domestic legal framework: 2017/2018

Summary of recommendations

Area of implementation	Recommendations for improvement
Domestic legal and administrative framework	None.
Exchange of information framework	None.
Appropriate use	None.

The domestic legal and administrative framework

Belgium confirms that its rules have not changed and continue to be applied effectively. Belgium continues to meet all terms of reference.[1]

The exchange of information framework

Belgium made some exchanges of CbC reports after the deadline. This was caused by a technical issue that has since been resolved and so no recommendation is required.

Belgium confirms that its rules have not changed and continue to be applied effectively. Belgium continues to meet all terms of reference.

Appropriate use of CbC reports

Belgium confirms that its rules have not changed and continue to be applied effectively. Belgium continues to meet all terms of reference.

Note

[1] Belgium's 2017/2018 review included a monitoring point relating to the rule according to which where there are more than one Constituent Entities of the same MNE Group that are resident for tax purposes in the EU, the MNE Group may designate one of such Constituent Entities to file the country-by-country report conforming to the requirements that would satisfy the filing requirement of all the Constituent Entities of such MNE Group that are resident for tax purposes in the EU. This monitoring point remains in place.

Belize

Overview of CbC reporting requirements

First reporting fiscal year: Commencing on or after 1 January 2019

Consolidated group revenue threshold: USD 850 million

Filing deadline: 12 months following the end of the reporting fiscal year

Local filing required: Yes

Surrogate parent entity filing permitted: Yes

First review of the domestic legal framework: 2019/2020

Summary of recommendations

Area of implementation	Recommendations for improvement
Domestic legal and administrative framework	It is recommended that Belize take steps to ensure that local filing only occurs in the circumstances permitted under the minimum standard.
Exchange of information framework	It is recommended that Belize take steps to implement processes or written procedures to ensure that the exchange of information is conducted in a manner consistent with the terms of reference relating to the exchange of information framework ahead of the first exchanges of information.
Appropriate use	Not reviewed.

The domestic legal and administrative framework

Belize has notified as a non-reciprocal jurisdiction and is therefore applying a local filing requirement more widely than is allowed by the standard. It is recommended that Belize take steps to ensure that local filing only occurs in the circumstances permitted under the minimum standard.

The exchange of information framework

It is recommended that Belize take steps to implement processes or written procedures to ensure that the exchange of information is conducted in a manner consistent with the terms of reference relating to the exchange of information framework. This recommendation remains in place since the 2017/2018 peer review.

Appropriate use of CbC reports

Belize is a non-reciprocal jurisdiction and, as such, will not receive CbC reports submitted to tax authorities in other jurisdictions, and will not apply local filing. It is not necessary for this peer review evaluation to reach any conclusion with respect to Belize's compliance with the terms of reference on appropriate use.

Benin

Overview of CbC reporting requirements

Benin has not yet introduced a requirement for the filing of CbC reports, as required under the BEPS Action 13 (CbC reporting) minimum standard.

Summary of recommendations

Area of implementation	Recommendations for improvement
Domestic legal and administrative framework	It is recommended that Benin take steps to implement a domestic legal and administrative framework to impose and enforce CbC requirements as soon as possible.
Exchange of information framework	It is recommended that Benin take steps to have qualifying competent authority agreements in effect with jurisdictions of the Inclusive Framework that meet the confidentiality, consistency and appropriate use conditions and with which Benin has an international exchange of information agreement in effect that allows for the automatic exchange of tax information It is recommended that Benin take steps to implement the necessary processes or written procedures to ensure that the exchange of information is conducted in a manner consistent with the terms of reference relating to the exchange of information framework.
Appropriate use	It is recommended that Benin take steps to ensure that the appropriate use condition is met ahead of the first exchanges of information.

The domestic legal and administrative framework

Benin does not yet have legislation in place to implement the BEPS Action 13 minimum standard.

It is recommended that Benin take steps to implement a domestic legal and administrative framework to impose and enforce CbC requirements as soon as possible. This recommendation remains in place since the 2017/2018 peer review.

The exchange of information framework

Benin has no bilateral relationships in place for the exchange of CbC reports nor processes to ensure that the exchange of information is conducted in a manner consistent with the terms of reference relating to the exchange of information framework.

It is recommended that Benin take steps to have qualifying competent authority agreements in effect with jurisdictions of the Inclusive Framework that meet the confidentiality, consistency and appropriate use conditions and with which Benin has an international exchange of information agreement in effect that allows for the automatic exchange of tax information. This recommendation remains in place since the 2017/2018 peer review.

It is recommended that Benin take steps to implement the necessary processes or written procedures to ensure that the exchange of information is conducted in a manner consistent with the terms of reference relating to the exchange of information framework. This recommendation remains in place since the 2018/2019 peer review.

Appropriate use of CbC reports

Benin does not yet have controls in place to ensure the appropriate use of CbC reports.

It is recommended that Benin take steps to ensure that the appropriate use condition is met ahead of the first exchanges of information. This recommendation remains in place since the 2017/2018 peer review.

Bermuda

Overview of CbC reporting requirements

First reporting fiscal year: Commencing on or after 1 January 2016

Consolidated group revenue threshold: EUR 750 million

Filing deadline: 12 months following the end of the reporting fiscal year

Local filing required: No

Surrogate parent entity filing permitted: Yes

First review of the domestic legal framework: 2017/2018

Summary of recommendations

Area of implementation	Recommendations for improvement
Domestic legal and administrative framework	None.
Exchange of information framework	None.
Appropriate use	Not reviewed.

The domestic legal and administrative framework

Bermuda confirms that its rules have not changed and continue to be applied effectively. Bermuda continues to meet all terms of reference.[1]

The exchange of information framework

Bermuda confirms that its rules have not changed and continue to be applied effectively. Bermuda continues to meet all terms of reference.

Appropriate use of CbC reports

Bermuda is a non-reciprocal jurisdiction and, as such, will not receive CbC reports submitted to tax authorities in other jurisdictions, and will not apply local filing. It is therefore not necessary for this peer review evaluation to reach any conclusions with respect to Bermuda's compliance with the terms of reference on appropriate use.

Note

[1] Bermuda's 2017/2018 peer review included a monitoring point relating to the interpretation of the definition of "Revenue – Unrelated Party" and "Revenue – Related Party". Bermuda has now issued revised guidance which clarifies these definitions but it has not been possible to carry out a review of this guidance. The monitoring point remains in place and this guidance will be reviewed as part of the next peer review.

Bosnia and Herzegovina

Overview of CbC reporting requirements

First reporting fiscal year: Commencing on or after 1 January 2018

Consolidated group revenue threshold: BAM 1.5 billion / EUR 750 million

Filing deadline: 31 March of year following reporting year

Local filing required: No

Surrogate parent entity filing permitted: Yes

First review of the domestic legal framework: 2019/2020

Summary of recommendations

Area of implementation	Recommendations for improvement
Domestic legal and administrative framework	It is recommended that Bosnia and Herzegovina take steps to ensure that the filing requirement for CbC reporting applies equally to all relevant entities with no exemptions. It is recommended that Bosnia and Herzegovina take steps to amend legislation or otherwise clarify that the threshold requirement applies in line with the standard. It is recommended that Bosnia and Herzegovina take steps to amend legislation or otherwise ensure that the filing deadline is not more than 12 months from the end of the reporting fiscal year. It is recommended that Bosnia and Herzegovina take steps to implement procedures to ensure compliance with their filing requirement.
Exchange of information framework	It is recommended that Bosnia and Herzegovina take steps to have qualifying competent authority agreements in effect with jurisdictions of the Inclusive Framework which meet the confidentiality, consistency and appropriate use conditions and with which Bosnia and Herzegovina has an international exchange of information agreement in effect that allows for the automatic exchange of tax information. It is recommended that Bosnia and Herzegovina take steps to implement the necessary processes or written procedures to ensure that the exchange of information is conducted in a manner consistent with the terms of reference relating to the exchange of information framework. It is recommended that Bosnia and Herzegovina take steps to ensure that the number of reports received and exchanged are monitored.
Appropriate use	It is recommended that Bosnia and Herzegovina take steps to ensure that the appropriate use condition is met.

The domestic legal and administrative framework

Bosnia and Herzegovina has filing requirements which apply inconsistently and which are not in line with the standard.

It is recommended that Bosnia and Herzegovina take steps to ensure that the filing requirement for CbC reporting applies equally to all relevant entities with no exemptions.

It is recommended that Bosnia and Herzegovina take steps to amend legislation or otherwise clarify that the threshold requirement applies in line with the standard.

It is recommended that Bosnia and Herzegovina take steps to amend legislation or otherwise ensure that the filing deadline is not more than 12 months from the end of the reporting fiscal year.

It is recommended that Bosnia and Herzegovina take steps to implement procedures to ensure compliance with their filing requirement.

These recommendations remain in place since the 2019/2020 peer review.

The exchange of information framework

Bosnia and Herzegovina has no bilateral relationships in place for the exchange of CbC reports nor processes to ensure that the exchange of information is conducted in a manner consistent with the terms of reference relating to the exchange of information framework.

It is recommended that Bosnia and Herzegovina take steps to have qualifying competent authority agreements in effect with jurisdictions of the Inclusive Framework which meet the confidentiality, consistency and appropriate use conditions and with which Bosnia and Herzegovina has an international exchange of information agreement in effect that allows for the automatic exchange of tax information.

It is recommended that Bosnia and Herzegovina take steps to implement the necessary processes or written procedures to ensure that the exchange of information is conducted in a manner consistent with the terms of reference relating to the exchange of information framework.

These recommendations remain in place since the 2019/2020 peer review.

Bosnia and Herzegovina has not supplied information on the reports it has received from MNE Groups and which it has exchanged on time. It is recommended that Bosnia and Herzegovina take steps to ensure that the number of reports received and exchanged are monitored.

Appropriate use of CbC reports

Bosnia and Herzegovina does not yet have controls in place to ensure the appropriate use of CbC reports.

It is recommended that Bosnia and Herzegovina take steps to ensure that the appropriate use condition is met. This recommendation remains in place since the 2019/2020 peer review.

Botswana

Overview of CbC reporting requirements

Botswana has not yet introduced a requirement for the filing of CbC reports, as required under the BEPS Action 13 (CbC reporting) minimum standard.

Summary of recommendations

Area of implementation	Recommendations for improvement
Domestic legal and administrative framework	It is recommended that Botswana take steps to implement a domestic legal and administrative framework to impose and enforce CbC reporting requirements as soon as possible.
Exchange of information framework	It is recommended that Botswana take steps to have qualifying competent authority agreements in effect with jurisdictions of the Inclusive Framework that meet the confidentiality, consistency and appropriate use conditions and with which Botswana has an international exchange of information agreement in effect that allows for the automatic exchange of tax information It is recommended that Botswana take steps to implement the necessary processes or written procedures to ensure that the exchange of information is conducted in a manner consistent with the terms of reference relating to the exchange of information framework.
Appropriate use	It is recommended that Botswana take steps to ensure that the appropriate use condition is met ahead of the first exchanges of information.

The domestic legal and administrative framework

Botswana does not yet have legislation in place to implement the BEPS Action 13 minimum standard.

It is recommended that Botswana take steps to implement a domestic legal and administrative framework to impose and enforce CbC reporting requirements as soon as possible. This recommendation remains in place since the 2018/2019 peer review.

The exchange of information framework

Botswana has no bilateral relationships in place for the exchange of CbC reports nor processes to ensure that the exchange of information is conducted in a manner consistent with the terms of reference relating to the exchange of information framework.

It is recommended that Botswana take steps to have qualifying competent authority agreements in effect with jurisdictions of the Inclusive Framework that meet the confidentiality, consistency and appropriate use conditions and with which Botswana has an international exchange of information agreement in effect that allows for the automatic exchange of tax information. This recommendation remains in place since the 2018/2019 peer review.

It is recommended that Botswana take steps to implement the necessary processes or written procedures to ensure that the exchange of information is conducted in a manner consistent with the terms of reference relating to the exchange of information framework. This recommendation remains in place since the 2018/2019 peer review.

Appropriate use of CbC reports

Botswana does not yet have controls in place to ensure the appropriate use of CbC reports.

It is recommended that Botswana take steps to ensure that the appropriate use condition is met ahead of the first exchanges of information. This recommendation remains in place since the 2018/2019 peer review.

Brazil

Overview of CbC reporting requirements

First reporting fiscal year: Commencing on or after 1 January 2016

Consolidated group revenue threshold: BRL 2,260 billion

Filing deadline: 7 months following the end of the reporting fiscal year

Local filing required: Yes

Surrogate parent entity filing permitted: Yes

First review of the domestic legal framework: 2017/2018

Summary of recommendations

Area of implementation	Recommendations for improvement
Domestic legal and administrative framework	None.
Exchange of information framework	None.
Appropriate use	None.

The domestic legal and administrative framework

Brazil confirms that its rules have not changed and continue to be applied effectively. Brazil continues to meet all terms of reference.[1]

The exchange of information framework

Brazil made some exchanges of CbC reports after the deadline. This was caused by a policy to stagger exchanges beginning on the day they are due. Brazil has changed its policy and will begin the staggered exchanges earlier and so no recommendation is required.

Brazil confirms that its rules have not changed and continue to be applied effectively. Brazil continues to meet all terms of reference.

Appropriate use of CbC reports

Brazil confirms that its rules have not changed and continue to be applied effectively. Brazil continues to meet all terms of reference.

Note

[1] Brazil's 2017/2018 peer review included a general monitoring point relating to a specific process that would allow it to take appropriate measures in case Brazil is notified by another jurisdiction that such other jurisdiction has reason to believe that an error may have led to incorrect or incomplete information reporting by a Reporting Entity or that there is non-compliance of a Reporting Entity with respect to its obligation to file a CbC report. This monitoring point remains in place.

British Virgin Islands

Overview of CbC reporting requirements

First reporting fiscal year: Commencing on or after 1 January 2018

Consolidated group revenue threshold: EUR 750 million

Filing deadline: 12 months following the end of the reporting fiscal year

Local filing required: No

Surrogate parent entity filing permitted: Yes

First review of the domestic legal framework: 2018/2019

Summary of recommendations

Area of implementation	Recommendations for improvement
Domestic legal and administrative framework	None.
Exchange of information framework	None.
Appropriate use	Not reviewed.

The domestic legal and administrative framework

British Virgin Islands confirms that its rules have not changed and continue to be applied effectively. British Virgin Islands continues to meet all terms of reference.

The exchange of information framework

British Virgin Islands 2020/2021 report included a recommendation that the British Virgin Islands take steps to implement processes or written procedures to ensure that the exchange of information is conducted in a manner consistent with the terms of reference relating to the exchange of information framework. Information on the implementation of these process has been provided and this recommendation is removed.

British Virgin Islands 2020/2021 report included a recommendation that British Virgin Islands take steps to ensure that the number of reports received and exchanged are monitored. This information has been provided for this review and this recommendation is removed.

Appropriate use of CbC reports

British Virgin Islands is a non-reciprocal jurisdiction and, as such, will not receive CbC reports submitted to tax authorities in other jurisdictions, and will not apply local filing. It is therefore not necessary for this peer review evaluation to reach any conclusions with respect to compliance with the terms of reference on appropriate use.

Brunei Darussalam

Overview of CbC reporting requirements

Brunei Darussalam has not yet introduced a requirement for the filing of CbC reports, as required under the BEPS Action 13 (CbC reporting) minimum standard.

Summary of recommendations

Area of implementation	Recommendations for improvement
Domestic legal and administrative framework	It is recommended that Brunei Darussalam take steps to implement a domestic legal and administrative framework to impose and enforce CbC reporting requirements as soon as possible.
Exchange of information framework	It is recommended that Brunei Darussalam take steps to have qualifying competent authority agreements in effect with jurisdictions of the Inclusive Framework that meet the confidentiality, consistency and appropriate use conditions and with which Brunei Darussalam has an international exchange of information agreement in effect that allows for the automatic exchange of tax information It is recommended that Brunei Darussalam take steps to implement the necessary processes or written procedures to ensure that the exchange of information is conducted in a manner consistent with the terms of reference relating to the exchange of information framework.
Appropriate use	It is recommended that Brunei Darussalam take steps to ensure that the appropriate use condition is met ahead of the first exchanges of information.

The domestic legal and administrative framework

Brunei Darussalam does not yet have legislation in place to implement the BEPS Action 13 minimum standard.

It is recommended that Brunei Darussalam take steps to implement a domestic legal and administrative framework to impose and enforce CbC reporting requirements as soon as possible. This recommendation remains in place since the 2017/2018 peer review.

The exchange of information framework

Brunei Darussalam has no bilateral relationships in place for the exchange of CbC reports nor processes to ensure that the exchange of information is conducted in a manner consistent with the terms of reference relating to the exchange of information framework.

It is recommended that Brunei Darussalam take steps to have qualifying competent authority agreements in effect with jurisdictions of the Inclusive Framework that meet the confidentiality, consistency and appropriate use conditions and with which Brunei Darussalam has an international exchange of information agreement in effect that allows for the automatic exchange of tax information. This recommendation remains in place since the 2017/2018 peer review.

It is recommended that Brunei Darussalam take steps to implement the necessary processes or written procedures to ensure that the exchange of information is conducted in a manner consistent with the terms of reference relating to the exchange of information framework. This recommendation remains in place since the 2018/2019 peer review.

Appropriate use of CbC reports

Brunei Darussalam does not yet have controls in place to ensure the appropriate use of CbC reports.

It is recommended that Brunei Darussalam take steps to ensure that the appropriate use condition is met ahead of the first exchanges of information. This recommendation remains in place since the 2017/2018 peer review.

Bulgaria

Overview of CbC reporting requirements

First reporting fiscal year: Commencing on or after 1 January 2016

Consolidated group revenue threshold: EUR 750 million

Filing deadline: 12 months following the end of the reporting fiscal year

Local filing required: Yes, for reporting fiscal years commencing on or after 1 January 2017

Surrogate parent entity filing permitted: Yes

First review of the domestic legal framework: 2017/2018

Summary of recommendations

Area of implementation	Recommendations for improvement
Domestic legal and administrative framework	It is recommended that Bulgaria take steps to ensure that local filing only occurs in the circumstances permitted under the minimum standard.
Exchange of information framework	None.
Appropriate use	Not reviewed.

The domestic legal and administrative framework

Bulgaria has notified as a non-reciprocal jurisdiction and is therefore applying a local filing requirement more widely than is allowed by the standard. It is recommended that Bulgaria take steps to ensure that local filing only occurs in the circumstances permitted under the minimum standard. This recommendation remains in place since the 2019/2020 peer review.

The exchange of information framework

Bulgaria confirms that its rules have not changed and continue to be applied effectively. Bulgaria continues to meet all terms of reference.

Bulgaria exchanged a number of reports late. This was caused by a temporary suspension of the report transmission system but as this issue has been resolved no recommendation is required.

Appropriate use of CbC reports

Bulgaria is a non-reciprocal jurisdiction and, as such, will not receive CbC reports submitted to tax authorities in other jurisdictions. It is therefore not necessary for this peer review evaluation to reach any conclusions with respect to Bulgaria's compliance with the terms of reference on appropriate use.

Cabo Verde

Overview of CbC reporting requirements

First reporting fiscal year: TBC

Consolidated group revenue threshold: EUR 750 million

Filing deadline: 12 months following the end of the reporting fiscal year

Local filing required: Yes

Surrogate parent entity filing permitted: No

First review of domestic legal framework: 2021/2022

Summary of recommendations

Area of implementation	Recommendations for improvement
Domestic legal and administrative framework	It is recommended that Cabo Verde amend the definition of effective date or otherwise clarify the definition to be in line with the standard. It is recommended that Cabo Verde take steps to ensure that local filing only occurs in the circumstances permitted under the minimum standard. It is recommended that Cabo Verde clarify that the annual consolidated group revenue threshold calculation rule applies in line with the OECD guidance on currency fluctuations in respect of an MNE Group whose Ultimate Parent Entity is located in a jurisdiction other than Cabo Verde. It is recommended that Cabo Verde publish the full content and format requirements of the CbC Report.
Exchange of information framework	It is recommended that Cabo Verde take steps to have qualifying competent authority agreements in effect with jurisdictions of the Inclusive Framework that meet the confidentiality, consistency and appropriate use conditions and with which Cabo Verde has an international exchange of information agreement in effect that allows for the automatic exchange of tax information. It is recommended that Cabo Verde take steps to implement the necessary processes or written procedures to ensure that the exchange of information is conducted in a manner consistent with the terms of reference relating to the exchange of information framework.
Appropriate use	It is recommended that Cabo Verde take steps to ensure that the appropriate use condition is met ahead of the first exchanges of information.

The domestic legal and administrative framework

Cabo Verde's 2020/2021 peer review confirmed that Cabo Verde has a legislative filing requirement in effect, but did not include a review of that legislation. Cabo Verde's legislation has now been reviewed.[1]

A legislative filing requirement is in effect which applies to all Ultimate Parent Entities of MNE Groups above a certain threshold and which required inclusion of all constituent entities.

A CbC reporting filing obligation applies in Cabo Verde and filing is required within 12 months after the reporting year end. Cabo Verde has enforcement requirements to ensure compliance with rules on CbC reporting.

There are a number of areas where there are recommendations to improve the legislation.

The definition of effective date

Cabo Verde's legislation does not include an effective date from which CbC reporting is requirement. It is recommended that Cabo Verde amend the legislation to include an effective date for the CbC filing requirement

The local filing provision

The local filing requirement in Cabo Verde's legislation applies to "The constituent entity…which is not the final parent entity of a group of multinational companies" and the legislative definition of multinational enterprise group does not specifically exclude groups which do not meet the threshold requirement. This can be read as requiring constituent entities of all multinational groups of any size to make a local filing if the conditions are met and is therefore too broad. It is recommended that Cabo Verde amend the definition of MNE groups to include a reference to MNE groups excluded by reference to the threshold, or to otherwise specify a threshold requirement for local filing.

The first condition in Cabo Verde's legislation for local filing says: "The constituent entity residing in Cape Verde…Are owned or controlled, directly or indirectly, by non-resident entities that are not required to submit an identical declaration". This is not in line with the condition to allow local filing, where the UPE of the group is not obligated to file a country-by-country report in its jurisdiction of tax residence. The condition contained in Cabo Verde's legislation is too broad, and can be read as covering situations such as where there is a filing requirement in the other jurisdiction but the ultimate parent entity is not caught by that requirement because it is below the threshold. The intention is that this condition should apply where there is no filing requirement, not just where the ultimate parent entity is not required to file. It is recommended that Cabo Verde amend the definition or otherwise clarify the definition to be in line with the standard.

Cabo Verde has a legislative requirement for local filing but which is in effect despite Cabo Verde not yet meeting all of the consistency, confidentiality and appropriate use conditions. It is therefore recommended that Cabo Verde take steps to ensure that local filing only occurs in the circumstances permitted under the minimum standard.

Currency Fluctuations

Where an MNE Group draws up, or would draw up, its Consolidated Financial Statements in a currency other than that specified by Cabo Verde, the reference to Cabo Verde's threshold has the effect as if it were a reference to the equivalent in that currency at the average exchange rate for the accounting period. While this provision would not create an issue for MNE Groups whose Ultimate Parent Entity is a tax resident in Cabo Verde, it may be incompatible with the guidance on currency fluctuations for MNE Groups whose Ultimate Parent Entity is located in another jurisdiction, if local filing requirements were applied in respect of a Constituent Entity (which is a Cabo Verde tax resident) of an MNE Group which does not reach the threshold as determined in the jurisdiction of the Ultimate Parent Entity of such a Group.

It is recommended that Cabo Verde clarify that the annual consolidated group revenue threshold calculation rule applies in line with the OECD guidance on currency fluctuations in respect of an MNE Group whose Ultimate Parent Entity is located in a jurisdiction other than Cabo Verde.

Contents of the Country-by-Country report

The information included in the legislative Annex does not include all of the template of the Country-by-Country report and does not include any details of what should be included under each heading in the report. It is recommended that Cabo Verde publish the full content and format requirements of the CbC Report.

The exchange of information framework

Cabo Verde has no bilateral relationships in place for the exchange of CbC reports nor processes to ensure that the exchange of information is conducted in a manner consistent with the terms of reference relating to the exchange of information framework.

It is recommended that Cabo Verde take steps to have qualifying competent authority agreements in effect with jurisdictions of the Inclusive Framework that meet the confidentiality, consistency and appropriate use conditions and with which Cabo Verde has an international exchange of information agreement in effect that allows for the automatic exchange of tax information. This recommendation remains in place since the 2019/2020 peer review.

It is recommended that Cabo Verde take steps to implement the necessary processes or written procedures to ensure that the exchange of information is conducted in a manner consistent with the terms of reference relating to the exchange of information framework. This recommendation remains in place since the 2019/2020 peer review.

Appropriate use of CbC reports

Cabo Verde does not yet have controls in place to ensure the appropriate use of CbC reports.

It is recommended that Cabo Verde take steps to ensure that the appropriate use condition is met ahead of the first exchanges of information. This recommendation remains in place since the 2019/2020 peer review.

Note

[1] https://www.mf.gov.cv/web/dnre/legislacao/-/document_library/kawUcttkhMXD/view_file/929559?_com_liferay_document_library_web_portlet_DLPortlet_INSTANCE_kawUcttkhMXD_redirect=https%3A%2F%2Fmf.gov.cv%2Fweb%2Fdnre%2Flegislacao%2F-%2Fdocument_library%2FkawUcttkhMXD%2Fview%2F64342%3F_com_liferay_document_library_web_portlet_DLPortlet_INSTANCE_kawUcttkhMXD_redirect%3Dhttps%253A%252F%252Fmf.gov.cv%252Fweb%252Fdnre%252Flegislacao%252F-%252Fdocument_library%252FkawUcttkhMXD%252Fview%252F63598.

Cameroon

Overview of CbC reporting requirements

Cameroon has not yet introduced a requirement for the filing of CbC reports, as required under the BEPS Action 13 (CbC reporting) minimum standard.

Summary of recommendations

Area of implementation	Recommendations for improvement
Domestic legal and administrative framework	It is recommended that Cameroon take steps to implement a domestic legal and administrative framework to impose and enforce CbC reporting requirements as soon as possible.
Exchange of information framework	It is recommended that Cameroon take steps to have qualifying competent authority agreements in effect with jurisdictions of the Inclusive Framework that meet the confidentiality, consistency and appropriate use conditions and with which Cameroon has an international exchange of information agreement in effect that allows for the automatic exchange of tax information. It is recommended that Cameroon take steps to implement the necessary processes or written procedures to ensure that the exchange of information is conducted in a manner consistent with the terms of reference relating to the exchange of information framework.
Appropriate use	It is recommended that Cameroon take steps to ensure that the appropriate use condition is met ahead of the first exchanges of information.

The domestic legal and administrative framework

Cameroon does not yet have legislation in place to implement the BEPS Action 13 minimum standard.

It is recommended that Cameroon take steps to implement a domestic legal and administrative framework to impose and enforce CbC reporting requirements as soon as possible. This recommendation remains in place since the 2017/2018 peer review.

The exchange of information framework

Cameroon has no bilateral relationships in place for the exchange of CbC reports nor processes to ensure that the exchange of information is conducted in a manner consistent with the terms of reference relating to the exchange of information framework.

It is recommended that Cameroon take steps to have qualifying competent authority agreements in effect with jurisdictions of the Inclusive Framework that meet the confidentiality, consistency and appropriate use conditions and with which Cameroon has an international exchange of information agreement in effect that allows for the automatic exchange of tax information. This recommendation remains in place since the 2017/2018 peer review.

It is recommended that Cameroon take steps to implement the necessary processes or written procedures to ensure that the exchange of information is conducted in a manner consistent with the terms of reference relating to the exchange of information framework. This recommendation remains in place since the 2018/2019 peer review.

Appropriate use of CbC reports

Cameroon does not yet have controls in place to ensure the appropriate use of CbC reports.

It is recommended that Cameroon take steps to ensure that the appropriate use condition is met ahead of the first exchanges of information. This recommendation remains in place since the 2017/2018 peer review.

Canada

Overview of CbC reporting requirements

First reporting fiscal year: Commencing on or after 1 January 2016

Consolidated group revenue threshold: EUR 750 million

Filing deadline: 12 months following the end of the reporting fiscal year

Local filing required: Yes

Surrogate parent entity filing permitted: Yes

First review of the domestic legal framework: 2017/2018

Summary of recommendations

Area of implementation	Recommendations for improvement
Domestic legal and administrative framework	None.
Exchange of information framework	None.
Appropriate use	None.

The domestic legal and administrative framework

Canada confirms that its rules have not changed and continue to be applied effectively. Canada continues to meet all terms of reference.

The exchange of information framework

Canada confirms that its rules have not changed and continue to be applied effectively. Canada continues to meet all terms of reference.

Appropriate use of CbC reports

Canada confirms that its rules have not changed and continue to be applied effectively. Canada continues to meet all terms of reference.

Cayman Islands

Overview of CbC reporting requirements

First reporting fiscal year: Commencing on or after 1 January 2016

Consolidated group revenue threshold: USD 850 million

Filing deadline: 12 months following the end of the reporting fiscal year

Local filing required: No

Surrogate parent entity filing permitted: Yes

First review of the domestic legal framework: 2017/2018

Summary of recommendations

Area of implementation	Recommendations for improvement
Domestic legal and administrative framework	None.
Exchange of information framework	None.
Appropriate use	Not reviewed.

The domestic legal and administrative framework

The Cayman Islands confirms that its rules have not changed and continue to be applied effectively. The Cayman Islands continues to meet all terms of reference.

The exchange of information framework

The Cayman Islands made some exchanges of CbC reports after the deadline. This was caused by a technical issue which has since been resolved and so no recommendation is required.

The Cayman Islands confirms that its rules have not changed and continue to be applied effectively. The Cayman Islands continues to meet all terms of reference.

Appropriate use of CbC reports

The Cayman Islands is a non-reciprocal jurisdiction and, as such, will not receive CbC reports submitted to tax authorities in other jurisdictions, and will not apply local filing. It is therefore not necessary for this peer review evaluation to reach any conclusions with respect to the Cayman Islands' compliance with the terms of reference on appropriate use.

Chile

Overview of CbC reporting requirements

First reporting fiscal year: Commencing on or after 1 January 2016

Consolidated group revenue threshold: EUR 750 million

Filing deadline: 6 months following the end of the reporting fiscal year

Local filing required: No

Surrogate parent entity filing permitted: Yes

First review of the domestic legal framework: 2017/2018

Summary of recommendations

Area of implementation	Recommendations for improvement
Domestic legal and administrative framework	None.
Exchange of information framework	None.
Appropriate use	None.

The domestic legal and administrative framework

Chile confirms that its rules have not changed and continue to be applied effectively. Chile continues to meet all terms of reference.

The exchange of information framework

Chile confirms that its rules have not changed and continue to be applied effectively. Chile continues to meet all terms of reference.

Appropriate use of CbC reports

Chile confirms that its rules have not changed and continue to be applied effectively. Chile continues to meet all terms of reference.

China (People's Republic of)

Overview of CbC reporting requirements

First reporting fiscal year: Commencing on or after 1 January 2016

Consolidated group revenue threshold: RMB 5.5 billion

Filing deadline: 5 months following the end of the reporting fiscal year

Local filing required: Yes

Surrogate parent entity filing permitted: Yes

First review of the domestic legal framework: 2017/2018

Summary of recommendations

Area of implementation	Recommendations for improvement
Domestic legal and administrative framework	It is recommendation that China clarify the exact scope, conditions and legal basis under the minimum standard and/or the exchange of information framework for the filing exemption in relation to information relating to National Security. It is recommended that China amend its legislation or otherwise takes steps to ensure that local filing is only required in the circumstances contained in the terms of reference.
Exchange of information framework	None.
Appropriate use	None.

The domestic legal and administrative framework

It is recommendation that China clarify the exact scope, conditions and legal basis under the minimum standard and/or the exchange of information framework for the filing exemption in relation to information relating to National Security. This recommendation remains in place since the 2017/2018 peer review.

It is recommended that China amend its legislation or otherwise takes steps to ensure that local filing is only required in the circumstances contained in the terms of reference. This recommendation remains in place since the 2017/2018 peer review.

The exchange of information framework

China's 2018/2019 included a recommendation that China implement a process to ensure that each of the mandatory fields of information required in the CbC reporting template are present in the information exchanged. China has introduced a system validation system that ensures all fields required in the CbC reporting template are included in the CbCR filing system and so this recommendation has been removed.

China made some exchanges of CbC reports after the deadline. This was is due to a technical issue with one particular batch of reports which has been resolved and no therefore no recommendation is required.

China confirms that its rules have not changed and continue to be applied effectively. China continues to meet all terms of reference.

Appropriate use of CbC reports

China confirms that its rules have not changed and continue to be applied effectively. China continues to meet all terms of reference.

Colombia

Overview of CbC reporting requirements

First reporting fiscal year: Commencing on or after 1 January 2016

Consolidated group revenue threshold: UVT 81 million (Tax Value Units)

Filing deadline: 12 months following the end of the reporting fiscal year

Local filing required: Yes

Surrogate parent entity filing permitted: Yes

First review of the domestic legal framework: 2017/2018

Summary of recommendations

Area of implementation	Recommendations for improvement
Domestic legal and administrative framework	None.
Exchange of information framework	None.
Appropriate use	None.

The domestic legal and administrative framework

Colombia confirms that its rules have not changed and continue to be applied effectively. Colombia continues to meet all terms of reference.

The exchange of information framework

Colombia confirms that its rules have not changed and continue to be applied effectively. Colombia continues to meet all terms of reference.

Appropriate use of CbC reports

Colombia confirms that its rules have not changed and continue to be applied effectively. Colombia continues to meet all terms of reference.

Congo

Overview of CbC reporting requirements

Congo has not yet introduced a requirement for the filing of CbC reports, as required under the BEPS Action 13 (CbC reporting) minimum standard.

Summary of recommendations

Area of implementation	Recommendations for improvement
Domestic legal and administrative framework	It is recommended that Congo take steps to implement a domestic legal and administrative framework to impose and enforce CbC reporting requirements as soon as possible.
Exchange of information framework	It is recommended that Congo take steps to have qualifying competent authority agreements in effect with jurisdictions of the Inclusive Framework that meet the confidentiality, consistency and appropriate use conditions and with which Congo has an international exchange of information agreement in effect that allows for the automatic exchange of tax information. It is recommended that Congo take steps to implement the necessary processes or written procedures to ensure that the exchange of information is conducted in a manner consistent with the terms of reference relating to the exchange of information framework.
Appropriate use	It is recommended that Congo take steps to ensure that the appropriate use condition is met ahead of the first exchanges of information.

The domestic legal and administrative framework

Congo does not yet have legislation in place to implement the BEPS Action 13 minimum standard.

It is recommended that Congo take steps to implement a domestic legal and administrative framework to impose and enforce CbC reporting requirements as soon as possible. This recommendation remains in place since the 2019/2020 peer review.

The exchange of information framework

Congo has no bilateral relationships in place for the exchange of CbC reports nor processes to ensure that the exchange of information is conducted in a manner consistent with the terms of reference relating to the exchange of information framework.

It is recommended that Congo take steps to have qualifying competent authority agreements in effect with jurisdictions of the Inclusive Framework that meet the confidentiality, consistency and appropriate use conditions and with which Congo has an international exchange of information agreement in effect that allows for the automatic exchange of tax information. This recommendation remains in place since the 2019/2020 peer review.

It is recommended that Congo take steps to implement the necessary processes or written procedures to ensure that the exchange of information is conducted in a manner consistent with the terms of reference relating to the exchange of information framework. This recommendation remains in place since the 2019/2020 peer review.

Appropriate use of CbC reports

Congo does not yet have controls in place to ensure the appropriate use of CbC reports.

It is recommended that Congo take steps to ensure that the appropriate use condition is met ahead of the first exchanges of information. This recommendation remains in place since the 2019/2020 peer review.

Costa Rica

Overview of CbC reporting requirements

First reporting fiscal year: Commencing on or after 1 January 2017

Consolidated group revenue threshold: EUR 750 million

Filing deadline: 31 December of the year following the reporting fiscal year

Local filing required: No

Surrogate parent entity filing permitted: Yes

First review of the domestic legal framework: 2017/2018

Summary of recommendations

Area of implementation	Recommendations for improvement
Domestic legal and administrative framework	None.
Exchange of information framework	It is recommended that Costa Rica take steps to have the necessary processes in place ahead of the first exchanges of CbC reports.
Appropriate use	Not reviewed.

The domestic legal and administrative framework

Costa Rica confirms that its rules have not changed and continue to be applied effectively. Costa Rica continues to meet all terms of reference.

The exchange of information framework

It is recommended that Costa Rica take steps to have the necessary processes in place to ensure timely and accurate exchange of CbC reports.

Appropriate use of CbC reports

Costa Rica has notified as a non-reciprocal jurisdiction and, as such, will not receive CbC reports submitted to tax authorities in other jurisdictions. It is therefore not necessary for this peer review evaluation to reach any conclusions with respect to Costa Rica's compliance with the terms of reference on appropriate use.

Côte d'Ivoire

Overview of CbC reporting requirements

First reporting fiscal year: Commencing on or after 1 January 2018

Consolidated group revenue threshold: XOF 49,967,750,000

Filing deadline: 12 months following the end of the reporting fiscal year

Local filing required: No

Surrogate parent entity filing permitted: Yes

First review of the domestic legal framework: 2017/2018

Summary of recommendations

Area of implementation	Recommendations for improvement
Domestic legal and administrative framework	None.
Exchange of information framework	It is recommended that Côte d'Ivoire take steps to have qualifying competent authority agreements in effect with jurisdictions of the Inclusive Framework which meet the confidentiality, consistency and appropriate use conditions and with which Côte d'Ivoire has an international exchange of information agreement in effect that allows for the automatic exchange of tax information. It is also recommended that Côte d'Ivoire have in place the necessary processes or written procedures to ensure that the exchange of information is conducted in a manner consistent with the terms of reference relating to the exchange of information framework.
Appropriate use	It is recommended that Côte d'Ivoire take steps to ensure that the appropriate use condition is met.

The domestic legal and administrative framework

Côte d'Ivoire confirms that its rules have not changes and continue to be applied effectively. Côte d'Ivoire continues to meet all terms of reference.[1]

The exchange of information framework

Côte d'Ivoire has no bilateral relationships in place for the exchange of CbC reports nor processes to ensure that the exchange of information is conducted in a manner consistent with the terms of reference relating to the exchange of information framework

It is recommended that Côte d'Ivoire take steps to have qualifying competent authority agreements in effect with jurisdictions of the Inclusive Framework which meet the confidentiality, consistency and appropriate use conditions and with which Côte d'Ivoire has an international exchange of information agreement in effect that allows for the automatic exchange of tax information. This recommendation remains in place since the 2017/2018 peer review.

It is recommended that Côte d'Ivoire have in place the necessary processes or written procedures to ensure that the exchange of information is conducted in a manner consistent with the terms of reference relating to the exchange of information framework. This recommendation remains in place since the 2018/2019 peer review.

Appropriate use of CbC reports

Côte d'Ivoire does not yet have controls in place to ensure the appropriate use of CbC reports. It is recommended that Côte d'Ivoire take steps to ensure that the appropriate use condition is met. This recommendation remains in place since the 2017/2018 peer review.

Note

[1] Côte d'Ivoire's 2017/2018 peer review included a general monitoring point relating to a specific process to that would allow to take appropriate measures in case Côte d'Ivoire is notified by another jurisdiction that such other jurisdiction has reason to believe that an error may have led to incorrect or incomplete information reporting by a Reporting Entity or that there is non-compliance of a Reporting Entity with respect to its obligation to file a CbC report. This monitoring point remains in place.

Croatia

Overview of CbC reporting requirements

First reporting fiscal year: Commencing on or after 1 January 2016

Consolidated group revenue threshold: EUR 750 million

Filing deadline: 12 months following the end of the reporting fiscal year

Local filing required: Yes, for reporting fiscal years commencing on or after 1 January 2017

Surrogate parent entity filing permitted: Yes

First review of the domestic legal framework: 2017/2018

Summary of recommendations

Area of implementation	Recommendations for improvement
Domestic legal and administrative framework	None.
Exchange of information framework	None.
Appropriate use	None.

The domestic legal and administrative framework

Croatia confirms that its rules have not changed and continue to be applied effectively. Croatia continues to meet all terms of reference.[1]

The exchange of information framework

Croatia confirms that its rules have not changed and continue to be applied effectively. Croatia continues to meet all terms of reference.

Appropriate use of CbC reports

Croatia confirms that its rules have not changed and continue to be applied effectively. Croatia continues to meet all terms of reference.

Note

[1] Croatia's 2017/2018 peer review included a monitoring point relating to the definition of "related enterprises". This monitoring point remains in place.

Curaçao

Overview of CbC reporting requirements

First reporting fiscal year: Commencing on or after 1 January 2018. Curaçao also allowed MNE Groups to file a CbC report on a voluntary basis, for reporting fiscal years commencing between 1 January 2016 and 31 December 2017.

Consolidated group revenue threshold: NAFI 1.5 billion

Filing deadline: 12 months following the end of the reporting fiscal year

Local filing required: No

Surrogate parent entity filing permitted: Yes

First review of the domestic legal framework: 2018/2019

Summary of recommendations

Area of implementation	Recommendations for improvement
Domestic legal and administrative framework	None.
Exchange of information framework	None.
Appropriate use	Not reviewed.

The domestic legal and administrative framework

Curaçao confirms that its rules have not changed and continue to be applied effectively. Curaçao continues to meet all terms of reference.

The exchange of information framework

Curaçao confirms that its rules have not changed and continue to be applied effectively. Curaçao continues to meet all terms of reference.

Appropriate use of CbC reports

Curaçao is a non-reciprocal jurisdiction and, as such, will not receive CbC reports submitted to tax authorities in other jurisdictions, and will not apply local filing. It is therefore not necessary for this peer review evaluation to reach any conclusions with respect to Curaçao's compliance with the terms of reference on appropriate use.

Czech Republic

Overview of CbC reporting requirements

First reporting fiscal year: Commencing on or after 1 January 2016

Consolidated group revenue threshold: EUR 750 million

Filing deadline: 12 months following the end of the reporting fiscal year

Local filing required: Yes, for reporting fiscal years commencing on or after 1 January 2017

Surrogate parent entity filing permitted: Yes

First review of the domestic legal framework: 2017/2018

Summary of recommendations

Area of implementation	Recommendations for improvement
Domestic legal and administrative framework	None.
Exchange of information framework	None.
Appropriate use	None.

The domestic legal and administrative framework

The Czech Republic confirms that its rules have not changed and continue to be applied effectively. The Czech Republic continues to meet all terms of reference.

The exchange of information framework

The Czech Republic confirms that its rules have not changed and continue to be applied effectively. The Czech Republic continues to meet all terms of reference.

Appropriate use of CbC reports

The Czech Republic confirms that its rules have not changed and continue to be applied effectively. The Czech Republic continues to meet all terms of reference.

Democratic Republic of the Congo

Overview of CbC reporting requirements

The Democratic Republic of the Congo has not yet introduced a requirement for the filing of CbC reports, as required under the BEPS Action 13 (CbC reporting) minimum standard.

Summary of recommendations

Area of implementation	Recommendations for improvement
Domestic legal and administrative framework	It is recommended that the Democratic Republic of the Congo take steps to implement a domestic legal and administrative framework to impose and enforce CbC reporting requirements as soon as possible.
Exchange of information framework	It is recommended that the Democratic Republic of the Congo take steps to have qualifying competent authority agreements in effect with jurisdictions of the Inclusive Framework that meet the confidentiality, consistency and appropriate use conditions and with which the Democratic Republic of the Congo has an international exchange of information agreement in effect that allows for the automatic exchange of tax information. It is recommended that the Democratic Republic of the Congo take steps to implement the necessary processes or written procedures to ensure that the exchange of information is conducted in a manner consistent with the terms of reference relating to the exchange of information framework.
Appropriate use	It is recommended that the Democratic Republic of the Congo take steps to ensure that the appropriate use condition is met ahead of the first exchanges of information.

The domestic legal and administrative framework

The Democratic Republic of the Congo does not yet have legislation in place to implement the BEPS Action 13 minimum standard.

It is recommended that the Democratic Republic of the Congo take steps to implement a domestic legal and administrative framework to impose and enforce CbC reporting requirements as soon as possible. This recommendation remains in place since the 2017/2018 peer review.

The exchange of information framework

The Democratic Republic of the Congo has no bilateral relationships in place for the exchange of CbC reports nor processes to ensure that the exchange of information is conducted in a manner consistent with the terms of reference relating to the exchange of information framework.

It is recommended that the Democratic Republic of the Congo take steps to have qualifying competent authority agreements in effect with jurisdictions of the Inclusive Framework that meet the confidentiality, consistency and appropriate use conditions and with which the Democratic Republic of the Congo has an international exchange of information agreement in effect that allows for the automatic exchange of tax information. This recommendation remains in place since the 2017/2018 peer review.

It is recommended that the Democratic Republic of the Congo take steps to implement the necessary processes or written procedures to ensure that the exchange of information is conducted in a manner consistent with the terms of reference relating to the exchange of information framework. This recommendation remains in place since the 2018/2019 peer review.

Appropriate use of CbC reports

The Democratic Republic of the Congo does not yet have controls in place to ensure the appropriate use of CbC reports.

It is recommended that the Democratic Republic of the Congo take steps to ensure that the appropriate use condition is met ahead of the first exchanges of information. This recommendation remains in place since the 2017/2018 peer review.

Denmark

Overview of CbC reporting requirements

First reporting fiscal year: Commencing on or after 1 January 2016

Consolidated group revenue threshold: DKK 5.6 billion

Filing deadline: 12 months following the end of the reporting fiscal year

Local filing required: Yes, for reporting fiscal years commencing on or after 1 January 2017

Surrogate parent entity filing permitted: Yes

First review of the domestic legal framework: 2017/2018

Summary of recommendations

Area of implementation	Recommendations for improvement
Domestic legal and administrative framework	None.
Exchange of information framework	None.
Appropriate use	None.

The domestic legal and administrative framework

Denmark confirms that its rules have not changed and continue to be applied effectively. Denmark continues to meet all terms of reference.

The exchange of information framework

Denmark confirms that its rules have not changed and continue to be applied effectively. Denmark continues to meet all terms of reference.

Appropriate use of CbC reports

Denmark confirms that its rules have not changed and continue to be applied effectively. Denmark continues to meet all terms of reference.

Djibouti

Overview of CbC reporting requirements

Djibouti has not yet introduced a requirement for the filing of CbC reports, as required under the BEPS Action 13 (CbC reporting) minimum standard.

Summary of recommendations

Area of implementation	Recommendations for improvement
Domestic legal and administrative framework	It is recommended that Djibouti take steps to implement a domestic legal and administrative framework to impose and enforce CbC reporting requirements as soon as possible.
Exchange of information framework	It is recommended that Djibouti take steps to have qualifying competent authority agreements in effect with jurisdictions of the Inclusive Framework that meet the confidentiality, consistency and appropriate use conditions and with which Djibouti has an international exchange of information agreement in effect that allows for the automatic exchange of tax information. It is recommended that Djibouti take steps to implement the necessary processes or written procedures to ensure that the exchange of information is conducted in a manner consistent with the terms of reference relating to the exchange of information framework.
Appropriate use	It is recommended that Djibouti take steps to ensure that the appropriate use condition is met ahead of the first exchanges of information.

The domestic legal and administrative framework

Djibouti does not yet have legislation in place to implement the BEPS Action 13 minimum standard.

It is recommended that Djibouti take steps to implement a domestic legal and administrative framework to impose and enforce CbC reporting requirements as soon as possible. This recommendation remains in place since the 2018/2019 peer review.

The exchange of information framework

Djibouti has no bilateral relationships in place for the exchange of CbC reports nor processes to ensure that the exchange of information is conducted in a manner consistent with the terms of reference relating to the exchange of information framework.

It is recommended that Djibouti take steps to have qualifying competent authority agreements in effect with jurisdictions of the Inclusive Framework that meet the confidentiality, consistency and appropriate use conditions and with which Djibouti has an international exchange of information agreement in effect that allows for the automatic exchange of tax information. This recommendation remains in place since the 2018/2019 peer review.

It is recommended that Djibouti take steps to implement the necessary processes or written procedures to ensure that the exchange of information is conducted in a manner consistent with the terms of reference relating to the exchange of information framework. This recommendation remains in place since the 2018/2019 peer review.

Appropriate use of CbC reports

Djibouti does not yet have controls in place to ensure the appropriate use of CbC reports.

It is recommended that Djibouti take steps to ensure that the appropriate use condition is met ahead of the first exchanges of information. This recommendation remains in place since the 2018/2019 peer review.

Dominica

Overview of CbC reporting requirements

Dominica has not yet introduced a requirement for the filing of CbC reports, as required under the BEPS Action 13 (CbC reporting) minimum standard.

Summary of recommendations

Area of implementation	Recommendations for improvement
Domestic legal and administrative framework	It is recommended that Dominica take steps to implement a domestic legal and administrative framework to impose and enforce CbC reporting requirements as soon as possible.
Exchange of information framework	It is recommended that Dominica take steps to have qualifying competent authority agreements in effect with jurisdictions of the Inclusive Framework that meet the confidentiality, consistency and appropriate use conditions and with which Dominica has an international exchange of information agreement in effect that allows for the automatic exchange of tax information. It is recommended that Dominica take steps to implement the necessary processes or written procedures to ensure that the exchange of information is conducted in a manner consistent with the terms of reference relating to the exchange of information framework.
Appropriate use	It is recommended that Dominica take steps to ensure that the appropriate use condition is met ahead of the first exchanges of information.

The domestic legal and administrative framework

Dominica does not yet have legislation in place to implement the BEPS Action 13 minimum standard.

It is recommended that Dominica take steps to implement a domestic legal and administrative framework to impose and enforce CbC reporting requirements as soon as possible. This recommendation remains in place since the 2019/2020 peer review.

The exchange of information framework

Dominica has no bilateral relationships in place for the exchange of CbC reports nor processes to ensure that the exchange of information is conducted in a manner consistent with the terms of reference relating to the exchange of information framework.

It is recommended that Dominica take steps to have qualifying competent authority agreements in effect with jurisdictions of the Inclusive Framework that meet the confidentiality, consistency and appropriate use conditions and with which Dominica has an international exchange of information agreement in effect that allows for the automatic exchange of tax information. This recommendation remains in place since the 2019/2020 peer review.

It is recommended that Dominica take steps to implement the necessary processes or written procedures to ensure that the exchange of information is conducted in a manner consistent with the terms of reference relating to the exchange of information framework. This recommendation remains in place since the 2019/2020 peer review.

Appropriate use of CbC reports

Dominica does not yet have controls in place to ensure the appropriate use of CbC reports.

It is recommended that Dominica take steps to ensure that the appropriate use condition is met ahead of the first exchanges of information. This recommendation remains in place since the 2019/2020 peer review.

Dominican Republic

Overview of CbC reporting requirements

First reporting fiscal year: Commencing on or after 1 January 2022

Consolidated group revenue threshold: DOP 38,800,000,000

Filing deadline: 12 months following the end of the reporting fiscal year

Local filing required: Yes

Surrogate parent entity filing permitted: Yes

First review of domestic legal framework: 2021/2022

Summary of recommendations

Area of implementation	Recommendations for improvement
Domestic legal and administrative framework	It is recommended that Dominican Republic take steps to ensure that local filing only occurs in the circumstances permitted under the minimum standard.
Exchange of information framework	It is recommended that Dominican Republic take steps to have qualifying competent authority agreements in effect with jurisdictions of the Inclusive Framework that meet the confidentiality, consistency and appropriate use conditions and with which the Dominican Republic has an international exchange of information agreement in effect that allows for the automatic exchange of tax information. It is recommended that Dominican Republic take steps to implement the necessary processes or written procedures to ensure that the exchange of information is conducted in a manner consistent with the terms of reference relating to the exchange of information framework.
Appropriate use	It is recommended that Dominican Republic take steps to ensure that the appropriate use condition is met ahead of the first exchanges of information.

The domestic legal and administrative framework

The Dominican Republic's 2020/2021 peer review confirmed that the Dominican Republic has a legislative filing requirement in effect, but did not include a review of that legislation. The Dominican Republic's legislation has now been reviewed.

The Dominican Republic has a legislative filing requirement which applies to all Ultimate Parent Entities of MNE Groups above a certain threshold and which requires inclusion of all constituent entities.[1] [2]

A CbC reporting filing obligation applies in the Dominican Republic for fiscal years commencing in 2022 and filing is required 12 months after the reporting year end. The Dominican Republic has enforcement requirements to ensure compliance with rules on CbC reporting.

There is one recommendation related to improving the legislation.

The local filing provision

The Dominican Republic has a legislative requirement for local filing which is in line with the standard but which is in effect despite the Dominican Republic not yet meeting all of the consistency, confidentiality and appropriate use conditions. It is therefore recommended that the Dominican Republic take steps to ensure that local filing only occurs in the circumstances permitted under the minimum standard.

The exchange of information framework

The Dominican Republic has no bilateral relationships in place for the exchange of CbC reports nor processes to ensure that the exchange of information is conducted in a manner consistent with the terms of reference relating to the exchange of information framework.

It is recommended that the Dominican Republic take steps to have qualifying competent authority agreements in effect with jurisdictions of the Inclusive Framework that meet the confidentiality, consistency and appropriate use conditions and with which the Dominican Republic has an international exchange of information agreement in effect that allows for the automatic exchange of tax information. This recommendation remains in place since the 2019/2020 peer review.

It is recommended that the Dominican Republic take steps to implement the necessary processes or written procedures to ensure that the exchange of information is conducted in a manner consistent with the terms of reference relating to the exchange of information framework. This recommendation remains in place since the 2019/2020 peer review.

Appropriate use of CbC reports

The Dominican Republic does not yet have controls in place to ensure the appropriate use of CbC reports.

It is recommended that the Dominican Republic take steps to ensure that the appropriate use condition is met ahead of the first exchanges of information. This recommendation remains in place since the 2019/2020 peer review.

Notes

[1] https://dgii.gov.do/legislacion/decretos/Documents/2021/Decreto%20256-21.pdf.

[2] https://dgii.gov.do/legislacion/normasGenerales/Documents/Otras%20Normas%20de%20Inter%C3%A9s/Norma08-21.pdf#search=reporte%20pais%20por%20pais.

Egypt

Overview of CbC reporting requirements

First reporting fiscal year: Ending on or after 31 December 2018

Consolidated group revenue threshold: EGP 3 billion

Filing deadline: 12 months following the end of the reporting fiscal year

Local filing required: No

Surrogate parent entity filing permitted: Yes

First review of the domestic legal framework: 2017/2018

Summary of recommendations

Area of implementation	Recommendations for improvement
Domestic legal and administrative framework	None.
Exchange of information framework	It is recommended that Egypt take steps to have qualifying competent authority agreements in effect with jurisdictions of the Inclusive Framework which meet the confidentiality, consistency and appropriate use conditions and with which Egypt has an international exchange of information agreement in effect that allows for the automatic exchange of tax information. It is recommended that Egypt take steps to implement processes or written procedures to ensure that the exchange of information is conducted in a manner consistent with the terms of reference relating to the exchange of information framework ahead of its first exchanges of information.
Appropriate use	It is recommended that Egypt take steps to ensure that the appropriate use condition is met.

The domestic legal and administrative framework

Egypt confirms that its rules have not changed and continue to be applied effectively. Egypt continues to meet all terms of reference.

The exchange of information framework

Egypt has no bilateral relationships in place for the exchange of CbC reports nor processes to ensure that the exchange of information is conducted in a manner consistent with the terms of reference relating to the exchange of information framework.

It is recommended that Egypt take steps to have qualifying competent authority agreements in effect with jurisdictions of the Inclusive Framework which meet the confidentiality, consistency and appropriate use conditions and with which Egypt has an international exchange of information agreement in effect that allows for the automatic exchange of tax information remains in place. This recommendation remains in place since the 2017/2018 peer review.

It is recommended that Egypt take steps to implement processes or written procedures to ensure that the exchange of information is conducted in a manner consistent with the terms of reference relating to the exchange of information framework ahead of its first exchanges of information. This recommendation remains in place since the 2018/2019 peer review.

Appropriate use of CbC reports

Egypt does not yet have controls in place to ensure the appropriate use of CbC reports. It is recommended that Egypt take steps to ensure that the appropriate use condition is met. This recommendation remains in place since the 2017/2018 peer review.

Estonia

Overview of CbC reporting requirements

First reporting fiscal year: Commencing on or after 1 January 2016

Consolidated group revenue threshold: EUR 750 million

Filing deadline: 12 months following the end of the reporting fiscal year

Local filing required: Yes, for reporting fiscal years commencing on or after 1 January 2017

Surrogate parent entity filing permitted: Yes

First review of the domestic legal framework: 2017/2018

Summary of recommendations

Area of implementation	Recommendations for improvement
Domestic legal and administrative framework	None.
Exchange of information framework	None.
Appropriate use	None.

The domestic legal and administrative framework

Estonia confirms that its rules have not changed and continue to be applied effectively. Estonia continues to meet all terms of reference.[1] [2]

The exchange of information framework

Estonia confirms that its rules have not changed and continue to be applied effectively. Estonia continues to meet all terms of reference.

Appropriate use of CbC reports

Estonia confirms that its rules have not changed and continue to be applied effectively. Estonia continues to meet all terms of reference.

Notes

[1] Estonia's 2017/2018 peer review included a monitoring point relating to the threshold calculation rule which would be applied in a manner consistent with the OECD guidance on currency fluctuations (paragraph 8 (a) ii. of the terms of reference). This monitoring point remains in place.

[2] Estonia's 2017/2018 peer review included a general monitoring point relating to a specific process that would allow Estonia to take appropriate measures in case Estonia is notified by another jurisdiction that such other jurisdiction has reason to believe that an error may have led to incorrect or incomplete information reporting by a Reporting Entity or that there is non-compliance of a Reporting Entity with respect to its obligation to file a CbC report. This monitoring point remains in place.

Eswatini (Kingdom of)

Overview of CbC reporting requirements

The Kingdom of Eswatini (Eswatini) has not yet introduced a requirement for the filing of CbC reports, as required under the BEPS Action 13 (CbC reporting) minimum standard.

Summary of recommendations

Area of implementation	Recommendations for improvement
Domestic legal and administrative framework	It is recommended that Eswatini take steps to implement a domestic legal and administrative framework to impose and enforce CbC reporting requirements as soon as possible.
Exchange of information framework	It is recommended that Eswatini take steps to have qualifying competent authority agreements in effect with jurisdictions of the Inclusive Framework that meet the confidentiality, consistency and appropriate use conditions and with which Eswatini has an international exchange of information agreement in effect that allows for the automatic exchange of tax information. It is recommended that Eswatini take steps to implement the necessary processes or written procedures to ensure that the exchange of information is conducted in a manner consistent with the terms of reference relating to the exchange of information framework.
Appropriate use	It is recommended that Eswatini take steps to ensure that the appropriate use condition is met ahead of the first exchanges of information.

The domestic legal and administrative framework

Eswatini does not yet have legislation in place to implement the BEPS Action 13 minimum standard.

It is recommended that Eswatini take steps to implement a domestic legal and administrative framework to impose and enforce CbC reporting requirements as soon as possible. This recommendation remains in place since the 2019/2020 peer review.

The exchange of information framework

Eswatini has no bilateral relationships in place for the exchange of CbC reports nor processes to ensure that the exchange of information is conducted in a manner consistent with the terms of reference relating to the exchange of information framework.

It is recommended that Eswatini take steps to have qualifying competent authority agreements in effect with jurisdictions of the Inclusive Framework that meet the confidentiality, consistency and appropriate use conditions and with which Eswatini has an international exchange of information agreement in effect that allows for the automatic exchange of tax information. This recommendation remains in place since the 2019/2020 peer review.

It is recommended that Eswatini take steps to implement the necessary processes or written procedures to ensure that the exchange of information is conducted in a manner consistent with the terms of reference relating to the exchange of information framework. This recommendation remains in place since the 2019/2020 peer review.

Appropriate use of CbC reports

Eswatini does not yet have controls in place to ensure the appropriate use of CbC reports.

It is recommended that Eswatini take steps to ensure that the appropriate use condition is met ahead of the first exchanges of information. This recommendation remains in place since the 2019/2020 peer review.

Faroe Islands

Overview of CbC reporting requirements

First reporting fiscal year: Commencing on or after 20 December 2019

Consolidated group revenue threshold: DKK 5.6 billion

Filing deadline: 12 months following the end of the reporting fiscal year

Local filing required: Yes

Surrogate parent entity filing permitted: Yes

First review of the domestic legal framework: 2019/2020

Summary of recommendations

Area of implementation	Recommendations for improvement
Domestic legal and administrative framework	It is recommended that the Faroe Islands take steps to amend legislation or otherwise clarify that an MNE Group should consider its requirement to file using the consolidated group revenue for its fiscal year immediately preceding a reporting fiscal year for comparison with the threshold. It is recommended that the Faroe Islands take steps to amend legislation or otherwise clarify that there are no exemptions form the filing requirement for MNE Groups who meet the threshold requirement in the Faroe Islands. It is recommended that the Faroe Islands take steps to amend legislation or otherwise clarify that a CbC report should be filed within 12 months of the end of the reporting period the report applies to. It is recommended that the Faroe Islands take steps to implement procedures to ensure effective implementation of the filing requirement.
Exchange of information framework	It is recommended that the Faroe Islands take steps to have qualifying competent authority agreements in effect with jurisdictions of the Inclusive Framework which meet the confidentiality, consistency and appropriate use conditions and with which the Faroe Islands has an international exchange of information agreement in effect that allows for the automatic exchange of tax information. It is recommended that the Faroe Islands take steps to implement processes or written procedures to ensure that the exchange of information is conducted in a manner consistent with the terms of reference relating to the exchange of information framework.
Appropriate use	It is recommended that the Faroe Islands take steps to ensure that the appropriate use condition is met ahead of the first exchanges of information.

The domestic legal and administrative framework

It is recommended that the Faroe Islands take steps to amend legislation or otherwise clarify that an MNE Group should consider its requirement to file using the consolidated group revenue of its fiscal year immediately preceding a reporting fiscal year for comparison with the threshold. This recommendation remains in place since the 2019/2020 peer review.

It is recommended that the Faroe Islands take steps to amend legislation or otherwise clarify that there are no exemptions from the filing requirement for MNE Groups who meet the threshold requirement in the Faroe Islands. This recommendation remains in place since the 2019/2020 peer review.

It is recommended that the Faroe Islands take steps to amend legislation or otherwise clarify that a CbC report should be filed within 12 months of the end of the reporting period the report applies to. This recommendation remains in place since the 2019/2020 peer review.

It is recommended that the Faroe Islands take steps to implement procedures to ensure effective implementation of the filing requirement. This recommendation remains in place since the 2019/2020 peer review.

The Faroes Island's 2019/2020 peer report recommended that steps be taken to clarify that the annual consolidated group revenue threshold calculation rule applies in line with the OECD guidance on currency fluctuations in respect of an MNE Group whose Ultimate Parent Entity is located in a jurisdiction other than the Faroe Islands. The tax authority of the Faroe Islands has updated its website to confirm this point and therefore this recommendation is removed.[1]

The exchange of information framework

Faroe Islands has no bilateral relationships in place for the exchange of CbC reports nor processes to ensure that the exchange of information is conducted in a manner consistent with the terms of reference relating to the exchange of information framework.

It is recommended that the Faroe Islands take steps to have qualifying competent authority agreements in effect with jurisdictions of the Inclusive Framework which meet the confidentiality, consistency and appropriate use conditions and with which the Faroe Islands has an international exchange of information agreement in effect that allows for the automatic exchange of tax information. This recommendation remains in place since the 2019/2020 peer review.

It is recommended that the Faroe Islands take steps to implement processes or written procedures to ensure that the exchange of information is conducted in a manner consistent with the terms of reference relating to the exchange of information framework. This recommendation remains in place since the 2019/2020 peer review.

Appropriate use of CbC reports

Faroe Islands does not yet have controls in place to ensure the appropriate use of CbC reports.

It is recommended that the Faroe Islands take steps to ensure that the appropriate use condition is met ahead of the first exchanges of information. This recommendation remains in place since the 2019/2020 peer review.

Note

[1] https://www.taks.fo/fo/vinna/skattur/land-fyri-land-fragreiding/.

Finland

Overview of CbC reporting requirements

First reporting fiscal year: Commencing on or after 1 January 2016

Consolidated group revenue threshold: EUR 750 million

Filing deadline: 12 months following the end of the reporting fiscal year

Local filing required: Yes

Surrogate parent entity filing permitted: Yes

First review of the domestic legal framework: 2017/2018

Summary of recommendations

Area of implementation	Recommendations for improvement
Domestic legal and administrative framework	None.
Exchange of information framework	None.
Appropriate use	None.

The domestic legal and administrative framework

Finland confirms that its rules have not changed and continue to be applied effectively. Finland continues to meet all terms of reference.

The exchange of information framework

Finland confirms that its rules have not changed and continue to be applied effectively. Finland continues to meet all terms of reference.

Appropriate use of CbC reports

Finland confirms that its rules have not changed and continue to be applied effectively. Finland continues to meet all terms of reference.

France

Overview of CbC reporting requirements

First reporting fiscal year: Commencing on or after 1 January 2016

Consolidated group revenue threshold: EUR 750 million

Filing deadline: 12 months following the end of the reporting fiscal year

Local filing required: Yes

Surrogate parent entity filing permitted: Yes

First review of the domestic legal framework: 2017/2018

Summary of recommendations

Area of implementation	Recommendations for improvement
Domestic legal and administrative framework	It is recommended that France ensure that local filing only occurs in the circumstances contained in the terms of reference.
Exchange of information framework	None.
Appropriate use	None.

The domestic legal and administrative framework

France's 2017/2018 peer report included a recommendation that France introduce a provision which would have an equivalent effect as the "deemed listing provision", i.e. ensuring that all entities that are not legally required to prepare Consolidated Financial Statements (whether under commercial / company law, or under regulations governing the relevant stock exchange / market, or other) be included in the scope of the parent entity filing obligation. France has since released guidance, which clarifies the requirement for such entities to file a CbC report, and this recommendation is therefore removed.[1]

It is recommended that France ensure that local filing only occurs in the circumstances contained in the terms of reference. This recommendation remains in place since the 2017/2018 peer review.[2]

The exchange of information framework

Peer input was received for France about missing or incomplete information in CbC reports sent to another jurisdiction. France has since introduced changes to its IT systems to ensure such missing or incomplete information will be identifiable in advance, and these changes will be effective in time for the next filing period. As France has taken steps to address this issue, no recommendation is required but this aspect will be monitored.

France confirms that its rules have not changed and continue to be applied effectively. France continues to meet all terms of reference.

Appropriate use of CbC reports

France confirms that its rules have not changed and continue to be applied effectively. France continues to meet all terms of reference.

Notes

[1] https://www.impots.gouv.fr/la-declaration-pays-par-pays.

[2] France's 2017/2018 peer review included a monitoring point with respect to the limitation of local filing to the instances of "Systemic Failure" as defined in paragraph 21 of the terms of reference. France confirms that its legislation implies that the obligations under the CbC MCAA are complied with (in particular the obligation for a prior consultation between Competent Authorities under Section 6 of the CbC MCAA) and will only apply local filing if there is a "Systemic Failure". This monitoring point remains in place.

Gabon

Overview of CbC reporting requirements

First reporting fiscal year: Commencing on or after 1 January 2017

Consolidated group revenue threshold: XOF 49,967,750,000

Filing deadline: 12 months following the end of the reporting fiscal year

Local filing required: Yes

Surrogate parent entity filing permitted: Yes

First review of the domestic legal framework: 2017/2018

Summary of recommendations

Area of implementation	Recommendations for improvement
Domestic legal and administrative framework	It is recommended that Gabon finalise its requirements, in particular to: • complete or introduce the definitions of "Constituent Entity", "Group" and "MNE Group" which appear to be incomplete or missing, and • define the requirements on the content of a CbC report.
Exchange of information framework	It is recommended that Gabon take steps to have qualifying competent authority agreements in effect with jurisdictions of the Inclusive Framework that meet the confidentiality, consistency and appropriate use conditions and with which Gabon has an international exchange of information agreement in effect that allows for the automatic exchange of tax information. It is recommended that Gabon take steps to implement the necessary processes or written procedures to ensure that the exchange of information is conducted in a manner consistent with the terms of reference relating to the exchange of information framework.
Appropriate use	It is recommended that Gabon take steps to ensure that the appropriate use condition is met ahead of the first exchanges of information.

The domestic legal and administrative framework

It is recommended that Gabon finalise its requirements particularly to:

- complete or introduce the definitions of "Constituent Entity", "Group" and "MNE Group" which appear to be incomplete or missing, and
- define the requirements on the content of a CbC report.

This recommendation remains in place since the 2017/2018 peer review.

The exchange of information framework

Gabon has no bilateral relationships in place for the exchange of CbC reports nor processes to ensure that the exchange of information is conducted in a manner consistent with the terms of reference relating to the exchange of information framework.

It is recommended that Gabon take steps to have qualifying competent authority agreements in effect with jurisdictions of the Inclusive Framework that meet the confidentiality, consistency and appropriate use conditions and with which Gabon has an international exchange of information agreement in effect that allows for the automatic exchange of tax information. This recommendation remains in place since the 2017/2018 peer review.

It is recommended that Gabon take steps to implement the necessary processes or written procedures to ensure that the exchange of information is conducted in a manner consistent with the terms of reference relating to the exchange of information framework. This recommendation remains in place since the 2018/2019 peer review.

Appropriate use of CbC reports

Gabon does not yet have controls in place to ensure the appropriate use of CbC reports.

It is recommended that Gabon take steps to ensure that the appropriate use condition is met ahead of the first exchanges of information. This recommendation remain in place since the 2017/2018 peer review.

Georgia

Overview of CbC reporting requirements

First reporting fiscal year:

Consolidated group revenue threshold: EUR 750m

Filing deadline: before 31 December in the year following the accounting year

Local filing required: No

Surrogate parent entity filing permitted: No

First review of the domestic legal framework: 2021/2022

Summary of recommendations

Area of implementation	Recommendations for improvement
Domestic legal and administrative framework	It is recommended that Georgia amend the legislation to include an effective date for the requirement to file CbC reports. It is recommended that Georgia introduce a definition for Group or otherwise clarify the definition to be in line with the standard. The report includes a recommendation that Georgia publish the full content and format requirements of the CbC Report. It is recommended that Georgia take steps to amend legislation or otherwise ensure that the filing deadline is not more than 12 months from the end of the reporting fiscal year.
Exchange of information framework	It is recommended that Georgia take steps to have qualifying competent authority agreements in effect with jurisdictions of the Inclusive Framework that meet the confidentiality, consistency and appropriate use conditions and with which Georgia has an international exchange of information agreement in effect that allows for the automatic exchange of tax information. It is recommended that Georgia take steps to implement the necessary processes or written procedures to ensure that the exchange of information is conducted in a manner consistent with the terms of reference relating to the exchange of information framework.
Appropriate use	It is recommended that Georgia take steps to ensure that the appropriate use condition is met ahead of the first exchanges of information.

The domestic legal and administrative framework

Georgia's 2017/2018 peer review confirmed that Georgia has a legislative filing requirement in effect, but did not include a review of that legislation. Georgia's legislation has now been reviewed.

As Georgia's legislation does not include an effective date, a legislative filing requirement is therefore not in effect in Georgia. Georgia should introduce an effective date in the legislation in order to give effect to the filing requirement.

There are a number of other areas where there are recommendations to improve the legislation.

The definition of Group

Georgia's legislation does not include a definition of a Group.

It is recommended that Georgia amend the legislation to include the definition of a Group in line with the standard.

Contents of the Country-by-Country report

The information included in Georgia's legislation does not include the template of the Country-by-Country report and does not include any details of what should be included under each heading in the report.

It is recommended that Georgia publish the full content and format requirements of the CbC Report.

Deadline for filing of the Country-by-Country report

The filing deadline for a report in Georgia is 31 December in the year following the reporting year. Where a reporting year ends between 1 January and 30 December this will mean that the filing deadline is more than 12 months after that reporting year-end.

It is recommended that Georgia take steps to amend legislation or otherwise ensure that the filing deadline is not more than 12 months from the end of the reporting fiscal year.

The exchange of information framework

Georgia has no bilateral relationships in place for the exchange of CbC reports nor processes to ensure that the exchange of information is conducted in a manner consistent with the terms of reference relating to the exchange of information framework.

It is recommended that Georgia take steps to have qualifying competent authority agreements in effect with jurisdictions of the Inclusive Framework that meet the confidentiality, consistency and appropriate use conditions and with which Georgia has an international exchange of information agreement in effect that allows for the automatic exchange of tax information. This recommendation remains in place since the 2017/2018 peer review.

It is recommended that Georgia take steps to implement the necessary processes or written procedures to ensure that the exchange of information is conducted in a manner consistent with the terms of reference relating to the exchange of information framework. This recommendation remains in place since the 2018/2019 peer review.

Appropriate use of CbC reports

Georgia does not yet have controls in place to ensure the appropriate use of CbC reports.

It is recommended that Georgia take steps to ensure that the appropriate use condition is met ahead of the first exchanges of information. This recommendation remains in place since the 2017/2018 peer review.

Germany

Overview of CbC reporting requirements

First reporting fiscal year: Commencing on or after 1 January 2016

Consolidated group revenue threshold: EUR 750 million

Filing deadline: 12 months following the end of the reporting fiscal year

Local filing required: Yes, for reporting fiscal years commencing on or after 1 January 2017

Surrogate parent entity filing permitted: Yes

First review of the domestic legal framework: 2017/2018

Summary of recommendations

Area of implementation	Recommendations for improvement
Domestic legal and administrative framework	None.
Exchange of information framework	None.
Appropriate use	None.

The domestic legal and administrative framework

Germany confirms that its rules have not changed and continue to be applied effectively. Germany continues to meet all terms of reference.

The exchange of information framework

Germany made some exchanges of CbC reports after the deadline. This was caused by a technical issue during a system update to the new XML Schema. This has since been resolved and exchanges are being made on time, so no recommendation is required. Some of the reports which were not exchanged during the technical issue are being converted to the new XML schema for exchange in July 2022 and this issue will be monitored.

Germany confirms that its rules have not changed and continue to be applied effectively. Germany continues to meet all terms of reference.

Appropriate use of CbC reports

Germany confirms that its rules have not changed and continue to be applied effectively. Germany continues to meet all terms of reference.

Gibraltar

Overview of CbC reporting requirements

First reporting fiscal year: Commencing on or after 1 January 2016

Consolidated group revenue threshold: EUR 750 million

Filing deadline: 12 months following the end of the reporting fiscal year

Local filing required: Yes, for reporting fiscal years commencing on or after 1 January 2017

Surrogate parent entity filing permitted: Yes

First review of the domestic legal framework: 2019/2020

Summary of recommendations

Area of implementation	Recommendations for improvement
Domestic legal and administrative framework	None.
Exchange of information framework	None.
Appropriate use	None.

The domestic legal and administrative framework

Gibraltar confirms that its rules have not changed and continue to be applied effectively. Gibraltar continues to meet all terms of reference.

The exchange of information framework

Gibraltar made some exchanges of CbC reports after the deadline. This was caused by a technical problem which has since been resolved and so no recommendation is required.

Gibraltar confirms that its rules have not changed and continue to be applied effectively. Gibraltar continues to meet all terms of reference.

Appropriate use of CbC reports

Gibraltar confirms that its rules have not changed and continue to be applied effectively. Gibraltar continues to meet all terms of reference.

Greece

Overview of CbC reporting requirements

First reporting fiscal year: Commencing on or after 1 January 2016

Consolidated group revenue threshold: EUR 750 million

Filing deadline: 12 months following the end of the reporting fiscal year

Local filing required: Yes

Surrogate parent entity filing permitted: Yes

First review of the domestic legal framework: 2017/2018

Summary of recommendations

Area of implementation	Recommendations for improvement
Domestic legal and administrative framework	None.
Exchange of information framework	None.
Appropriate use	None.

The domestic legal and administrative framework

Greece confirms that its rules have not changed and continue to be applied effectively. Greece continues to meet all terms of reference.[1]

The exchange of information framework

Peer input was received for Greece about missing or incomplete information in CbC reports sent to another jurisdiction. Greece has since introduced changes to its IT systems to ensure such missing or incomplete information will be identifiable in advance, and these changes will be effective in time for the next exchange of reports. As Greece has taken steps to address this issue, no recommendation is made but this aspect will be monitored.

Greece confirms that its rules have not changed and continue to be applied effectively. Greece continues to meet all terms of reference.

Appropriate use of CbC reports

Greece confirms that its rules have not changed and continue to be applied effectively. Greece continues to meet all terms of reference.

Note

[1] Greece's 2017/2018 peer review included a general monitoring point relating to a specific process that would allow Greece to take appropriate measures in case Greece is notified by another jurisdiction that such other jurisdiction has reason to believe that an error may have led to incorrect or incomplete information reporting by a Reporting Entity or that there is non-compliance of a Reporting Entity with respect to its obligation to file a CbC report. This monitoring point remains in place.

Greenland

Overview of CbC reporting requirements

First reporting fiscal year: Commencing on or after 1 January 2019

Consolidated group revenue threshold: DKK 5.6 billion

Filing deadline: 12 months following the end of the reporting fiscal year

Local filing required: Yes

Surrogate parent entity filing permitted: Yes

First review of the domestic legal framework: 2019/2020

Summary of recommendations

Area of implementation	Recommendations for improvement
Domestic legal and administrative framework	It is recommended that Greenland clarify that the annual consolidated group revenue threshold calculation rule applies in line with the OECD guidance on currency fluctuations in respect of an MNE Group whose Ultimate Parent Entity is located in a jurisdiction other than Greenland.
Exchange of information framework	It is recommended that Greenland take steps to have qualifying competent authority agreements in effect with jurisdictions of the Inclusive Framework which meet the confidentiality, consistency and appropriate use conditions and with which Greenland has an international exchange of information agreement in effect that allows for the automatic exchange of tax information. It is recommended that Greenland take steps to implement processes or written procedures to ensure that the exchange of information is conducted in a manner consistent with the terms of reference relating to the exchange of information framework.
Appropriate use	It is recommended that Greenland take steps to ensure that the appropriate use condition is met ahead of the first exchanges of information.

The domestic legal and administrative framework

It is recommended that Greenland clarify that the annual consolidated group revenue threshold calculation rule applies in line with the OECD guidance on currency fluctuations in respect of an MNE Group whose Ultimate Parent Entity is located in a jurisdiction other than Greenland. This recommendation remains in place since the 2019/2020 peer review.

The exchange of information framework

Greenland has no bilateral relationships in place for the exchange of CbC reports nor processes to ensure that the exchange of information is conducted in a manner consistent with the terms of reference relating to the exchange of information framework.

It is recommended that Greenland take steps to have QCAAs in effect with jurisdictions of the Inclusive Framework which meet the confidentiality, consistency and appropriate use conditions and with which Greenland has an international exchange of information agreement in effect that allows for the automatic exchange of tax information. This recommendation remains in place since the 2019/2020 peer review.

It is recommended that Greenland take steps to implement processes or written procedures to ensure that the exchange of information is conducted in a manner consistent with the terms of reference relating to the exchange of information framework. This recommendation remains in place since the 2019/2020 peer review.

Appropriate use of CbC reports

Greenland does not yet have controls in place to ensure the appropriate use of CbC reports.

It is recommended that Greenland take steps to ensure that the appropriate use condition is met ahead of the first exchanges of information. This recommendation remains in place since the 2019/2020 peer review.

Grenada

Overview of CbC reporting requirements

Grenada has not yet introduced a requirement for the filing of CbC reports, as required under the BEPS Action 13 (CbC reporting) minimum standard.

Summary of recommendations

Area of implementation	Recommendations for improvement
Domestic legal and administrative framework	It is recommended that Grenada take steps to implement a domestic legal and administrative framework to impose and enforce CbC reporting requirements as soon as possible.
Exchange of information framework	It is recommended that Grenada take steps to have qualifying competent authority agreements in effect with jurisdictions of the Inclusive Framework that meet the confidentiality, consistency and appropriate use conditions and with which Grenada has an international exchange of information agreement in effect that allows for the automatic exchange of tax information. It is recommended that Grenada take steps to implement the necessary processes or written procedures to ensure that the exchange of information is conducted in a manner consistent with the terms of reference relating to the exchange of information framework.
Appropriate use	It is recommended that Grenada take steps to ensure that the appropriate use condition is met ahead of the first exchanges of information.

The domestic legal and administrative framework

Grenada does not yet have legislation in place to implement the BEPS Action 13 minimum standard.

It is recommended that Grenada take steps to implement a domestic legal and administrative framework to impose and enforce CbC reporting requirements as soon as possible. This recommendation remains in place since the 2019/2020 peer review.

The exchange of information framework

Grenada has no bilateral relationships in place for the exchange of CbC reports nor processes to ensure that the exchange of information is conducted in a manner consistent with the terms of reference relating to the exchange of information framework.

It is recommended that Grenada take steps to have qualifying competent authority agreements in effect with jurisdictions of the Inclusive Framework that meet the confidentiality, consistency and appropriate use conditions and with which Grenada has an international exchange of information agreement in effect that allows for the automatic exchange of tax information. This recommendation remains in place since the 2019/2020 peer review.

It is recommended that Grenada take steps to implement the necessary processes or written procedures to ensure that the exchange of information is conducted in a manner consistent with the terms of reference relating to the exchange of information framework. This recommendation remains in place since the 2019/2020 peer review.

Appropriate use of CbC reports

Grenada does not yet have controls in place to ensure the appropriate use of CbC reports.

It is recommended that Grenada take steps to ensure that the appropriate use condition is met ahead of the first exchanges of information. This recommendation remains in place since the 2019/2020 peer review.

Guernsey

Overview of CbC reporting requirements

First reporting fiscal year: Commencing on or after 1 January 2016

Consolidated group revenue threshold: EUR 750 million

Filing deadline: 12 months following the end of the reporting fiscal year

Local filing required: Yes

Surrogate parent entity filing permitted: Yes

First review of the domestic legal framework: 2017/2018

Summary of recommendations

Area of implementation	Recommendations for improvement
Domestic legal and administrative framework	None.
Exchange of information framework	None.
Appropriate use	None.

The domestic legal and administrative framework

Guernsey confirms that its rules have not changed and continue to be applied effectively. Guernsey continues to meet all terms of reference.[1]

The exchange of information framework

Guernsey confirms that its rules have not changed and continue to be applied effectively. Guernsey continues to meet all terms of reference.

Appropriate use of CbC reports

Guernsey confirms that its rules have not changed and continue to be applied effectively. Guernsey continues to meet all terms of reference.

Note

[1] Guernsey's 2017/2018 peer review included a general monitoring point relating to a specific process that would allow Guernsey to take appropriate measures in case Guernsey is notified by another jurisdiction that such other jurisdiction has reason to believe that an error may have led to incorrect or incomplete information reporting by a Reporting Entity or that there is non-compliance of a Reporting Entity with respect to its obligation to file a CbC report. This monitoring point remains in place.

Haiti

Overview of CbC reporting requirements

Haiti has not yet introduced a requirement for the filing of CbC reports, as required under the BEPS Action 13 (CbC reporting) minimum standard.

Summary of recommendations

Area of implementation	Recommendations for improvement
Domestic legal and administrative framework	It is recommended that Haiti take steps to implement a domestic legal and administrative framework to impose and enforce CbC reporting requirements as soon as possible.
Exchange of information framework	It is recommended that Haiti take steps to have qualifying competent authority agreements in effect with jurisdictions of the Inclusive Framework that meet the confidentiality, consistency and appropriate use conditions and with which Haiti has an international exchange of information agreement in effect that allows for the automatic exchange of tax information It is recommended that Haiti take steps to implement the necessary processes or written procedures to ensure that the exchange of information is conducted in a manner consistent with the terms of reference relating to the exchange of information framework.
Appropriate use	It is recommended that Haiti take steps to ensure that the appropriate use condition is met ahead of the first exchanges of information.

The domestic legal and administrative framework

Haiti does not yet have legislation in place to implement the BEPS Action 13 minimum standard.

It is recommended that Haiti take steps to implement a domestic legal and administrative framework to impose and enforce CbC reporting requirements as soon as possible. This recommendation remains in place since the 2017/2018 peer review.

The exchange of information framework

Haiti has no bilateral relationships in place for the exchange of CbC reports nor processes to ensure that the exchange of information is conducted in a manner consistent with the terms of reference relating to the exchange of information framework.

It is recommended that Haiti take steps to have qualifying competent authority agreements in effect with jurisdictions of the Inclusive Framework that meet the confidentiality, consistency and appropriate use conditions and with which Haiti has an international exchange of information agreement in effect that allows for the automatic exchange of tax information. This recommendation remains in place since the 2017/2018 peer review.

It is recommended that Haiti take steps to implement the necessary processes or written procedures to ensure that the exchange of information is conducted in a manner consistent with the terms of reference relating to the exchange of information framework. This recommendation remains in place since the 2018/2019 peer review.

Appropriate use of CbC reports

Haiti does not yet have controls in place to ensure the appropriate use of CbC reports.

It is recommended that Haiti take steps to ensure that the appropriate use condition is met ahead of the first exchanges of information. This recommendation remains in place since the 2017/2018 peer review.

Honduras

Overview of CbC reporting requirements

Honduras has not yet introduced a requirement for the filing of CbC reports, as required under the BEPS Action 13 (CbC reporting) minimum standard.

Summary of recommendations

Area of implementation	Recommendations for improvement
Domestic legal and administrative framework	It is recommended that Honduras take steps to implement a domestic legal and administrative framework to impose and enforce CbC reporting requirements as soon as possible.
Exchange of information framework	It is recommended that Honduras take steps to have qualifying competent authority agreements in effect with jurisdictions of the Inclusive Framework that meet the confidentiality, consistency and appropriate use conditions and with which Honduras has an international exchange of information agreement in effect that allows for the automatic exchange of tax information. It is recommended that Honduras take steps to implement the necessary processes or written procedures to ensure that the exchange of information is conducted in a manner consistent with the terms of reference relating to the exchange of information framework.
Appropriate use	It is recommended that Honduras take steps to ensure that the appropriate use condition is met ahead of the first exchanges of information.

The domestic legal and administrative framework

Honduras does not yet have legislation in place to implement the BEPS Action 13 minimum standard.

It is recommended that Honduras take steps to implement a domestic legal and administrative framework to impose and enforce CbC reporting requirements as soon as possible. This recommendation remains in place since the 2020/2021 peer review.

The exchange of information framework

Honduras has no bilateral relationships in place for the exchange of CbC reports nor processes to ensure that the exchange of information is conducted in a manner consistent with the terms of reference relating to the exchange of information framework.

It is recommended that Honduras take steps to have qualifying competent authority agreements in effect with jurisdictions of the Inclusive Framework that meet the confidentiality, consistency and appropriate use conditions and with which Honduras has an international exchange of information agreement in effect that allows for the automatic exchange of tax information. This recommendation remains in place since the 2020/2021 peer review.

It is recommended that Honduras take steps to implement the necessary processes or written procedures to ensure that the exchange of information is conducted in a manner consistent with the terms of reference relating to the exchange of information framework. This recommendation remains in place since the 2020/2021 peer review.

Appropriate use of CbC reports

Honduras does not yet have controls in place to ensure the appropriate use of CbC reports.

It is recommended that Honduras take steps to ensure that the appropriate use condition is met ahead of the first exchanges of information. This recommendation remains in place since the 2020/2021 peer review.

Hong Kong

Overview of CbC reporting requirements

First reporting fiscal year: Commencing on or after 1 January 2018. Hong Kong also allowed MNE Groups to file a CbC report on a voluntary basis, for reporting fiscal years commencing between 1 January 2016 and 31 December 2017.

Consolidated group revenue threshold: HKD 6.8 billion

Filing deadline: 12 months following the end of the reporting fiscal year

Local filing required: Yes

Surrogate parent entity filing permitted: Yes

First review of the domestic legal framework: 2018/2019

Summary of recommendations

Area of implementation	Recommendations for improvement
Domestic legal and administrative framework	None.
Exchange of information framework	None.
Appropriate use	None.

The domestic legal and administrative framework

Hong Kong confirms that its rules have not changed and continue to be applied effectively. Hong Kong continues to meet all terms of reference.

The exchange of information framework

Hong Kong confirms that its rules have not changed and continue to be applied effectively. Hong Kong continues to meet all terms of reference.

Appropriate use of CbC reports

Hong Kong confirms that its rules have not changed and continue to be applied effectively. Hong Kong continues to meet all terms of reference.

Hungary

Overview of CbC reporting requirements

First reporting fiscal year: Commencing on or after 1 January 2016

Consolidated group revenue threshold: EUR 750 million

Filing deadline: 12 months following the end of the reporting fiscal year

Local filing required: Yes, for reporting fiscal years commencing on or after 1 January 2017

Surrogate parent entity filing permitted: Yes

First review of the domestic legal framework: 2017/2018

Summary of recommendations

Area of implementation	Recommendations for improvement
Domestic legal and administrative framework	None.
Exchange of information framework	None.
Appropriate use	None.

The domestic legal and administrative framework

Hungary confirms that its rules have not changed and continue to be applied effectively. Hungary continues to meet all terms of reference.

The exchange of information framework

Hungary confirms that its rules have not changed and continue to be applied effectively. Hungary continues to meet all terms of reference.

Appropriate use of CbC reports

Hungary confirms that its rules have not changed and continue to be applied effectively. Hungary continues to meet all terms of reference.

Iceland

Overview of CbC reporting requirements

First reporting fiscal year: Commencing on or after 1 January 2017

Consolidated group revenue threshold: ISK 100 billion

Filing deadline: 12 months following the end of the reporting fiscal year

Local filing required: Yes

Surrogate parent entity filing permitted: Yes

First review of the domestic legal framework: 2017/2018

Summary of recommendations

Area of implementation	Recommendations for improvement
Domestic legal and administrative framework	None.
Exchange of information framework	None.
Appropriate use	None.

The domestic legal and administrative framework

In its 2017/2018 peer review, it was recommended that Iceland amend or otherwise clarify the definition of 'Ultimate Parent Entity" in a manner consistent with the definition contained in the terms of reference. Iceland has made a legislative change and this recommendation is therefore removed.[1] [2] [3]

The exchange of information framework

Iceland confirms that its rules have not changed and continue to be applied effectively. Iceland continues to meet all terms of reference.

Appropriate use of CbC reports

Iceland confirms that its rules have not changed and continue to be applied effectively. Iceland continues to meet all terms of reference.

Notes

[1] https://www.stjornartidindi.is/Advert.aspx?RecordID=929ac988-caf5-4bf7-b5d4-48f594cc7cd8.

[2] Iceland's 2017/2018 peer review included a monitoring point in relation to the issuance of updated interpretation or clarification of "Revenues – Related Party" within a reasonable timeframe to ensure consistency with OECD guidance. Iceland indicates it is in the process of updating existing guidance. This monitoring point remains in place.

[3] Iceland's 2017/2018 peer review included a general monitoring point relating to a specific process that would allow it to take appropriate measures in case Iceland is notified by another jurisdiction that such other jurisdiction has reason to believe that an error may have led to incorrect or incomplete information reporting by a Reporting Entity or that there is non-compliance of a Reporting Entity with respect to its obligation to file a CbC report. This monitoring point remains in place.

India

Overview of CbC reporting requirements

First reporting fiscal year: Commencing on or after 1 April 2016

Consolidated group revenue threshold: INR 50,500 million

Filing deadline: 12 months following the end of the reporting fiscal year

Local filing required: Yes

Surrogate parent entity filing permitted: Yes

First review of the domestic legal framework: 2017/2018

Summary of recommendations

Area of implementation	Recommendations for improvement
Domestic legal and administrative framework	It is recommended that India amend or otherwise clarify that the annual consolidated group revenue threshold calculation rule applies in a manner consistent with the OECD guidance on currency fluctuations in respect of an MNE Group whose Ultimate Parent Entity is located in a jurisdiction other than India. It is recommended that India amend its legislation or otherwise takes steps to ensure that local filing only occurs in the circumstances permitted under the minimum standard.
Exchange of information framework	None.
Appropriate use	None.

The domestic legal and administrative framework

It is recommended that India amend or otherwise clarify that the annual consolidated group revenue threshold calculation rule applies in a manner consistent with the OECD guidance on currency fluctuations in respect of an MNE Group whose Ultimate Parent Entity is located in a jurisdiction other than India. This recommendation remains in place since the 2017/2018 peer review.

It is recommended that India amend its legislation or otherwise takes steps ensure that local filing only occurs in the circumstances permitted under the minimum standard. This recommendation remains in place since the 2017/2018 peer review.

The exchange of information framework

India confirms that its rules have not changed and continue to be applied effectively. India continues to meet all terms of reference.

Appropriate use of CbC reports

India confirms that its rules have not changed and continue to be applied effectively. India continues to meet all terms of reference.

Indonesia

Overview of CbC reporting requirements

First reporting fiscal year: Commencing on or after 1 January 2016

Consolidated group revenue threshold: IDR 11 trillion

Filing deadline: 12 months following the end of the reporting fiscal year

Local filing required: Yes

Surrogate parent entity filing permitted: Yes

First review of the domestic legal framework: 2017/2018

Summary of recommendations

Area of implementation	Recommendations for improvement
Domestic legal and administrative framework	None.
Exchange of information framework	None.
Appropriate use	None.

The domestic legal and administrative framework

Indonesia confirms that its rules have not changed and continue to be applied effectively. Indonesia continues to meet all terms of reference.[1] [2]

The exchange of information framework

Indonesia confirms that its rules have not changed and continue to be applied effectively. Indonesia continues to meet all terms of reference.

Appropriate use of CbC reports

Indonesia confirms that its rules have not changed and continue to be applied effectively. Indonesia continues to meet all terms of reference.

Notes

[1] Indonesia's 2017/2018 peer review included a monitoring point in relation to the local filing in case of "systemic failure". This monitoring point remains in place.

[2] Indonesia's 2017/2018 peer review included a monitoring point in relation to one of the conditions to deactivate the local filing obligation in case of surrogate filing. This monitoring point remains in place.

Ireland

Overview of CbC reporting requirements

First reporting fiscal year: Commencing on or after 1 January 2016

Consolidated group revenue threshold: EUR 750 million

Filing deadline: 12 months following the end of the reporting fiscal year

Local filing required: Yes

Surrogate parent entity filing permitted: Yes

First review of the domestic legal framework: 2017/2018

Summary of recommendations

Area of implementation	Recommendations for improvement
Domestic legal and administrative framework	None.
Exchange of information framework	None.
Appropriate use	None.

The domestic legal and administrative framework

Ireland confirms that its rules have not changed and continue to be applied effectively. Ireland continues to meet all terms of reference.[1]

The exchange of information framework

Ireland confirms that its rules have not changed and continue to be applied effectively. Ireland continues to meet all terms of reference.

Appropriate use of CbC reports

Ireland confirms that its rules have not changed and continue to be applied effectively. Ireland continues to meet all terms of reference.

Note

[1] Ireland's 2017/2018 peer review included a monitoring point relating to the conditions under which local filing may be required (paragraph 8 (c) iv. b) of the terms of reference). This monitoring point remains in place.

Isle of Man

Overview of CbC reporting requirements

First reporting fiscal year: Commencing on or after 1 January 2017. The Isle of Man also allowed MNE Groups to file a CbC report on a voluntary basis, for reporting fiscal years commencing between 1 January 2016 and 31 December 2016.

Consolidated group revenue threshold: EUR 750 million

Filing deadline: 12 months and one day following the end of the reporting fiscal year

Local filing required: Yes

Surrogate parent entity filing permitted: Yes

First review of the domestic legal framework: 2017/2018

Summary of recommendations

Area of implementation	Recommendations for improvement
Domestic legal and administrative framework	None.
Exchange of information framework	None.
Appropriate use	None.

The domestic legal and administrative framework

The Isle of Man confirms that its rules have not changed and continue to be applied effectively. The Isle of Man continues to meet all terms of reference.

The exchange of information framework

The Isle of Man confirms that its rules have not changed and continue to be applied effectively. The Isle of Man continues to meet all terms of reference.

Appropriate use of CbC reports

The Isle of Man confirms that its rules have not changed and continue to be applied effectively. The Isle of Man continues to meet all terms of reference.

Israel

Overview of CbC reporting requirements

Israel has not yet introduced a requirement for the filing of CbC reports, as required under the BEPS Action 13 (CbC reporting) minimum standard.

Summary of recommendations

Area of implementation	Recommendations for improvement
Domestic legal and administrative framework	A review of Israel's domestic legal and administrative framework will be included in the next peer review report.
Exchange of information framework	It is recommended that Israel take steps to have qualifying competent authority agreements in effect with jurisdictions of the Inclusive Framework that meet the confidentiality, consistency and appropriate use conditions and with which Israel has an international exchange of information agreement in effect that allows for the automatic exchange of tax information It is recommended that Israel take steps to implement the necessary processes or written procedures to ensure that the exchange of information is conducted in a manner consistent with the terms of reference relating to the exchange of information framework.
Appropriate use	It is recommended that Israel take steps to ensure that the appropriate use condition is met ahead of the first exchanges of information.

The domestic legal and administrative framework

Israel's 2020/2021 peer review report included a recommendation to take steps to implement legislation to impose a CbC reporting filing requirement. Israel has since introduced such a filing requirement but it has not been possible to carry out a review of this legislation. The recommendation to implement legislation is therefore removed and a review of the legislation will take place in the next peer review.

The exchange of information framework

Israel has no bilateral relationships in place for the exchange of CbC reports nor processes to ensure that the exchange of information is conducted in a manner consistent with the terms of reference relating to the exchange of information framework.

It is recommended that Israel take steps to have qualifying competent authority agreements in effect with jurisdictions of the Inclusive Framework that meet the confidentiality, consistency and appropriate use conditions and with which Israel has an international exchange of information agreement in effect that allows for the automatic exchange of tax information

It is recommended that Israel take steps to implement the necessary processes or written procedures to ensure that the exchange of information is conducted in a manner consistent with the terms of reference relating to the exchange of information framework.

Appropriate use of CbC reports

Israel does not yet have controls in place to ensure the appropriate use of CbC reports.

It is recommended that Israel take steps to ensure that the appropriate use condition is met ahead of the first exchanges of information.

Italy

Overview of CbC reporting requirements

First reporting fiscal year: Commencing on or after 1 January 2016

Consolidated group revenue threshold: EUR 750 million

Filing deadline: 12 months following the end of the reporting fiscal year

Local filing required: Yes

Surrogate parent entity filing permitted: Yes

First review of the domestic legal framework: 2017/2018

Summary of recommendations

Area of implementation	Recommendations for improvement
Domestic legal and administrative framework	None.
Exchange of information framework	None.
Appropriate use	None.

The domestic legal and administrative framework

Italy confirms that its rules have not changed and continue to be applied effectively. Italy continues to meet all terms of reference.

The exchange of information framework

Italy confirms that its rules have not changed and continue to be applied effectively. Italy continues to meet all terms of reference.

Appropriate use of CbC reports

Italy confirms that its rules have not changed and continue to be applied effectively. Italy continues to meet all terms of reference.

Jamaica

Overview of CbC reporting requirements

Jamaica has not yet introduced a requirement for the filing of CbC reports, as required under the BEPS Action 13 (CbC reporting) minimum standard.

Summary of recommendations

Area of implementation	Recommendations for improvement
Domestic legal and administrative framework	It is recommended that Jamaica take steps to implement a domestic legal and administrative framework to impose and enforce CbC reporting requirements as soon as possible.
Exchange of information framework	It is recommended that Jamaica take steps to have qualifying competent authority agreements in effect with jurisdictions of the Inclusive Framework that meet the confidentiality, consistency and appropriate use conditions and with which Jamaica has an international exchange of information agreement in effect that allows for the automatic exchange of tax information. It is recommended that Jamaica take steps to implement the necessary processes or written procedures to ensure that the exchange of information is conducted in a manner consistent with the terms of reference relating to the exchange of information framework.
Appropriate use	It is recommended that Jamaica take steps to ensure that the appropriate use condition is met ahead of the first exchanges of information.

The domestic legal and administrative framework

Jamaica does not yet have legislation in place to implement the BEPS Action 13 minimum standard.

It is recommended that Jamaica take steps to implement a domestic legal and administrative framework to impose and enforce CbC reporting requirements as soon as possible. This recommendation remains in place since the 2018/2019 peer review.

The exchange of information framework

Jamaica has no bilateral relationships in place for the exchange of CbC reports nor processes to ensure that the exchange of information is conducted in a manner consistent with the terms of reference relating to the exchange of information framework.

It is recommended that Jamaica take steps to have qualifying competent authority agreements in effect with jurisdictions of the Inclusive Framework that meet the confidentiality, consistency and appropriate use conditions and with which Jamaica has an international exchange of information agreement in effect that allows for the automatic exchange of tax information. This recommendation remains in place since the 2018/2019 peer review.

It is recommended that Jamaica take steps to implement the necessary processes or written procedures to ensure that the exchange of information is conducted in a manner consistent with the terms of reference relating to the exchange of information framework. This recommendation remains in place since the 2018/2019 peer review.

Appropriate use of CbC reports

Jamaica does not yet have controls in place to ensure the appropriate use of CbC reports.

It is recommended that Jamaica take steps to ensure that the appropriate use condition is met ahead of the first exchanges of information. This recommendation remains in place since the 2018/2019 peer review.

Japan

Overview of CbC reporting requirements

First reporting fiscal year: Commencing on or after 1 April 2016. Japan also allowed MNE Groups to file a CbC report on a voluntary basis, for reporting fiscal years commencing between 1 January 2016 and 31 March 2016.

Consolidated group revenue threshold: JPY 100 billion

Filing deadline: 12 months following the end of the reporting fiscal year

Local filing required: Yes. Transitional relief from local filing requirements applied to the fiscal year 1 April 2016 to 31 March 2017, except for the case where local filing arose as a result of a Systemic Failure by another jurisdiction.

Surrogate parent entity filing permitted: Yes

First review of the domestic legal framework: 2017/2018

Summary of recommendations

Area of implementation	Recommendations for improvement
Domestic legal and administrative framework	None.
Exchange of information framework	None.
Appropriate use	None.

The domestic legal and administrative framework

Japan confirms that its rules have not changed and continue to be applied effectively. Japan continues to meet all terms of reference.

The exchange of information framework

Japan confirms that its rules have not changed and continue to be applied effectively. Japan continues to meet all terms of reference.

Appropriate use of CbC reports

Japan confirms that its rules have not changed and continue to be applied effectively. Japan continues to meet all terms of reference.

Jersey

Overview of CbC reporting requirements

First reporting fiscal year: Commencing on or after 1 January 2016

Consolidated group revenue threshold: EUR 750 million

Filing deadline: 12 months following the end of the reporting fiscal year

Local filing required: Yes

Surrogate parent entity filing permitted: Yes

First review of the domestic legal framework: 2017/2018

Summary of recommendations

Area of implementation	Recommendations for improvement
Domestic legal and administrative framework	None.
Exchange of information framework	None.
Appropriate use	None.

The domestic legal and administrative framework

Jersey confirms that its rules have not changed and continue to be applied effectively. Jersey continues to meet all terms of reference.

The exchange of information framework

Jersey made some exchanges of CbC reports after the deadline due to technical issues around the change to XML Schema v2. These issues have been resolved, and so no recommendation is required.

Jersey confirms that its rules have not changed and continue to be applied effectively. Jersey continues to meet all terms of reference.

Appropriate use of CbC reports

Jersey confirms that its rules have not changed and continue to be applied effectively. Jersey continues to meet all terms of reference.

Jordan

Overview of CbC reporting requirements

First reporting fiscal year: Beginning on or after 1 January 2021

Consolidated group revenue threshold: JOD 600,000,000

Filing deadline: Within 12 ¾ months following the end of the reporting fiscal year

Local filing required: Yes

Surrogate parent entity filing permitted: Yes

First review of domestic legal framework: 2021/2022

Summary of recommendations

Area of implementation	Recommendations for improvement
Domestic legal and administrative framework	It is recommended that Jordan take steps to amend legislation or otherwise ensure that the filing deadline is not more than 12 months from the end of the reporting fiscal year. It is recommended that Jordan amend legislation or otherwise ensure that requirements on the sources of data that can be used in completing the CbC report template are in line with the standard. It is recommended that Jordan take steps to amend legislation or otherwise ensure that the form and content required in the CbC Report is in line with the standard. It is recommended that Jordan introduce or complete the definitions of a " "Group", "MNE Group", "Ultimate Parent Entity", "Constituent Entity", "Consolidated Financial Statements", "Fiscal Year", "Reporting Fiscal Year", "Reporting Entity", "Qualifying Competent Authority Agreement", "Surrogate Parent Entity", "Systemic Failure" and "International Agreement" in a manner that is consistent with the terms of reference. It is recommended that Jordan take steps to ensure that local filing only occurs in the circumstances permitted under the minimum standard. It is recommended that Jordan implement a provision whereby a single Constituent Entity of the same MNE Group may be designated to file the CbC report which would satisfy the local filing requirement of all the Constituent Entities in Jordan. It is recommended that Jordan clarify the circumstances in which surrogate entity filing is permitted. It is recommended that Jordan clarify that the annual consolidated group revenue threshold calculation rule applies in line with the OECD guidance on currency fluctuations in respect of an MNE Group whose Ultimate Parent Entity is located in a jurisdiction other than Jordan.
Exchange of information framework	It is recommended that Jordan take steps to have qualifying competent authority agreements in effect with jurisdictions of the Inclusive Framework that meet the confidentiality, consistency and appropriate use conditions and with which Jordan has an international exchange of information agreement in effect that allows for the automatic exchange of tax information. It is recommended that Jordan take steps to implement the necessary processes or written procedures to ensure that the exchange of information is conducted in a manner consistent with the terms of reference relating to the exchange of information framework.
Appropriate use	It is recommended that Jordan take steps to ensure that the appropriate use condition is met ahead of the first exchanges of information.

The domestic legal and administrative framework

Jordan's 2020/2021 peer review report included a recommendation to take steps to implement legislation to impose a CbC reporting filing requirement. Jordan has since introduced such a filing requirement and this recommendation is removed.[1]

A CbC reporting filing obligation applies in Jordan for fiscal years beginning on or after 1 January 2021 and filing is required 12 ¾ months after the reporting year end. Jordan has enforcement requirements to ensure compliance with rules on CbC reporting.

There are a number of areas where there are recommendations to improve the legislation.

Timing of parent entity filing

Jordan has a filing deadline for the CbC report that is 12 ¾ months after the year end. It is recommended that Jordan take steps to amend the legislation or otherwise ensure that the filing deadline is not more than 12 months from the end of the reporting fiscal year.

Use of audited consolidated financial statements as the source of data

Jordan's legislation specifies that the MNE Group must use audited consolidated financial statements in order to prepare the CbC report. Under the standard, an MNE Group may choose to use data from its consolidation reporting packages, from separate entity statutory financial statements, regulatory financial statements or internal management accounts and there is no requirement for financial statements to be audited. It is recommended that Jordan amend legislation or otherwise ensure that requirements on the sources of data that can be used in completing the CbC report template are in line with the standard.

Content of CbC Report

Jordan's legislation outlines the form and content of the CbC Report but requires more details in respect of income breakdown than is permitted under the standard. It is recommended that Jordan take steps to amend legislation or otherwise ensure that the form and content required in the CbC Report is in line with the standard.

The definition of Group

Jordan's legislation does not include a definition of "Group". It is recommended that Jordan amend its legislation to include a definition of "Group" that is in line with the standard.

The definition of MNE Group

The definition in Jordan's legislation refers to two or more related legal persons whose tax residence is in different countries, where those legal persons are considered a taxable person in their respective country of tax residence.

The definition of MNE Group should include businesses which are subject to tax in different jurisdictions through being taxable through a permanent establishment. It is recommended that Jordan amend the definition of MNE Group or otherwise clarify the definition to be in line with the standard.

The definition of Ultimate Parent Entity

The definition in Jordan's legislation refers to an entity that directly or indirectly owns stakes or shares in one or more multinational companies. The definition requires that the UPE is committed to preparing consolidated financial statements in accordance with international accounting standards generally accepted in the country in which it is tax resident.

The use of the term "committed" in Jordan's legislation, when referring to preparing consolidated financial statements, could be read as being optional. The definition in Jordan's legislation does not adequately capture the *requirement* to prepare consolidated financial statements, as is required under the standard.

Furthermore, the definition in Jordan's legislation also fails to cover circumstances where an entity owns directly or indirectly a sufficient interest in one or more other Constituent Entities such that it would required to prepare Consolidated Financial Statements if its equity interests were traded on a public securities exchange in its jurisdiction of tax residence (the "deemed listing provision"), which is required under the standard.

Finally, the definition in Jordan's legislation does not include the condition that no other Constituent Entity of the MNE Group owns directly or indirectly an interest described the first mentioned Constituent Entity.

It is recommended that Jordan amend the definition of UPE or otherwise clarify the definition to be in line with the standard.

The definition of Constituent Entity

Jordan's legislation does not include a definition of "Constituent Entity". It is recommended that Jordan amend its legislation to include a definition of "Constituent Entity" that is in line with the standard.

The definition of Consolidated Financial Statements

Jordan's legislation does not include a definition of "Consolidated Financial Statements". It is recommended that Jordan amend its legislation to include a definition of "Consolidated Financial Statements" that is in line with the standard.

The definition of Fiscal Year

Jordan's legislation does not include a definition of "Fiscal Year". It is recommended that Jordan amend its legislation to include a definition of "Fiscal Year" that is in line with the standard.

The definition of Reporting Fiscal Year

Jordan's legislation does not include a definition of "Reporting Fiscal Year". It is recommended that Jordan amend its legislation to include a definition of "Reporting Fiscal Year" that is in line with the standard.

The definition of Reporting Entity

The definition in Jordan's legislation refers to the taxpayer who submits the CbC report for each country to the relevant tax administration, on behalf of the MNE Group.

This definition does not outline who may be the Reporting Entity, for example the UPE, the Surrogate Parent Entity, or any other entity described in the legislation. Furthermore, it does not outline which entity is required to file the CbC report. It is recommended that Jordan amend the definition of Reporting Entity or otherwise clarify the definition to be in line with the standard.

The definition of Qualifying Competent Authority Agreement

Jordan's legislation does not include a definition of "Qualifying Competent Authority Agreement". It is recommended that Jordan amend its legislation to include a definition of "Qualifying Competent Authority Agreement" that is in line with the standard.

The definition of Surrogate Parent Entity

The definition in Jordan's legislation refers to the taxpayer affiliated with an MNE Group that is required to submit the CbC report to the department on behalf of the MNE Group.

The definition of Surrogate Parent Entity in the standard is intended to capture that the entity in question has been appointed by the MNE Group, as the sole substitute of the CbC Report, and only where certain conditions have been met (see below). It is recommended that Jordan amend the definition of Surrogate Parent Entity or otherwise clarify the definition to be in line with the standard.

The definition of Systemic Failure

Jordan's legislation does not include a definition of "Systemic Failure". It is recommended that Jordan amend its legislation to include a definition of "Systemic Failure" that is in line with the standard.

The definition of International Agreement

Jordan's legislation does not include a definition of "International Agreement". It is recommended that Jordan amend its legislation to include a definition of "International Agreement" that is in line with the standard.

The local filing provision

The local filing definition in Jordan's guidance applies to "a branch of this group in Jordan", meaning the MNE Group. The guidance does not include any further detail in respect of the circumstances under which local filing can take place. Furthermore, Jordan has a legislative requirement which is in effect despite Jordan not yet meeting all of the consistency, confidentiality and appropriate use conditions. It is therefore recommended that Jordan take steps to ensure that local filing only occurs in the circumstances permitted under the minimum standard.

Single entity filing

It is recommended that Jordan implement a provision whereby a single Constituent Entity of the same MNE Group may be designated to file the CbC report which would satisfy the local filing requirement of all the Constituent Entities in Jordan.

The surrogate filing provision

Jordan's guidance makes reference to a surrogate parent entity (see above), but does not include any further detail in respect of the circumstances under which surrogate filing is permitted. It is recommended that Jordan clarify the circumstances in which surrogate entity filing is permitted.

Currency Fluctuations

Where an MNE Group draws up, or would draw up, its Consolidated Financial Statements in a currency other than that specified by Jordan, the reference to Jordan's threshold has the effect as if it were a reference to the equivalent in that currency at the average exchange rate for the accounting period. While this provision would not create an issue for MNE Groups whose Ultimate Parent Entity is a tax resident in Jordan, it may be incompatible with the guidance on currency fluctuations for MNE Groups whose Ultimate Parent Entity is located in another jurisdiction, if local filing requirements were applied in respect of a Constituent Entity (which is a Jordan tax resident) of an MNE Group which does not reach the threshold as determined in the jurisdiction of the Ultimate Parent Entity of such a Group.

It is recommended that Jordan clarify that the annual consolidated group revenue threshold calculation rule applies in line with the OECD guidance on currency fluctuations in respect of an MNE Group whose Ultimate Parent Entity is located in a jurisdiction other than Jordan.

The exchange of information framework

Jordan has no bilateral relationships in place for the exchange of CbC reports nor processes to ensure that the exchange of information is conducted in a manner consistent with the terms of reference relating to the exchange of information framework.

It is recommended that Jordan take steps to have qualifying competent authority agreements in effect with jurisdictions of the Inclusive Framework that meet the confidentiality, consistency and appropriate use conditions and with which Jordan has an international exchange of information agreement in effect that allows for the automatic exchange of tax information. This recommendation remains in place since the 2019/2020 peer review.

It is recommended that Jordan take steps to implement the necessary processes or written procedures to ensure that the exchange of information is conducted in a manner consistent with the terms of reference relating to the exchange of information framework. This recommendation remains in place since the 2019/2020 peer review.

Appropriate use of CbC reports

Jordan does not yet have controls in place to ensure the appropriate use of CbC reports.

It is recommended that Jordan take steps to ensure that the appropriate use condition is met ahead of the first exchanges of information. This recommendation remains in place since the 2019/2020 peer review.

Note

[1] https://istd.gov.jo/Ar/List/%D8%AF%D9%84%D9%8A%D9%84_%D8%A7%D9%84%D8%AE%D8%AF%D9%85%D8%A7%D8%AA.

Kazakhstan

Overview of CbC reporting requirements

First reporting fiscal year: Commencing on or after 1 January 2016

Consolidated group revenue threshold: EUR 750 million

Filing deadline: 12 months following the end of the reporting fiscal year

Local filing required: Requirement suspended

Surrogate parent entity filing permitted: Yes

First review of the domestic legal framework: 2018/2019

Summary of recommendations

Area of implementation	Recommendations for improvement
Domestic legal and administrative framework	None.
Exchange of information framework	It is recommended that Kazakhstan take steps to implement processes or written procedures to ensure that the exchange of information is conducted in a manner consistent with the terms of reference relating to the exchange of information framework ahead of its first exchanges of information.
Appropriate use	It is recommended that Kazakhstan take steps to ensure that the appropriate use condition is met ahead of the first exchanges of information.

The domestic legal and administrative framework

Kazakhstan confirms that its rules have not changed and continue to be applied effectively. Kazakhstan continues to meet all terms of reference.

The exchange of information framework

It is recommended that Kazakhstan take steps to implement processes or written procedures to ensure that the exchange of information is conducted in a manner consistent with the terms of reference relating to the exchange of information framework ahead of its first exchanges of information. This recommendation remains in place since the 2018/2019 peer review.

Appropriate use of CbC reports

Previous peer review reports did not evaluate Kazakhstan's compliance with respect to appropriate use of CbC reports as Kazakhstan was a non-reciprocal jurisdiction. Kazakhstan is now a reciprocal jurisdiction and does not yet have controls in place to ensure the appropriate use of CbC reports.

It is recommended that Kazakhstan takes steps to ensure that the appropriate use condition is met ahead of the first exchanges of information.

Kenya

Overview of CbC reporting requirements

Kenya has not yet introduced a requirement for the filing of CbC reports, as required under the BEPS Action 13 (CbC reporting) minimum standard.

Summary of recommendations

Area of implementation	Recommendations for improvement
Domestic legal and administrative framework	It is recommended that Kenya take steps to implement a domestic legal and administrative framework to impose and enforce CbC reporting requirements as soon as possible.
Exchange of information framework	It is recommended that Kenya take steps to have qualifying competent authority agreements in effect with jurisdictions of the Inclusive Framework that meet the confidentiality, consistency and appropriate use conditions and with which Kenya has an international exchange of information agreement in effect that allows for the automatic exchange of tax information. It is recommended that Kenya take steps to implement the necessary processes or written procedures to ensure that the exchange of information is conducted in a manner consistent with the terms of reference relating to the exchange of information framework.
Appropriate use	It is recommended that Kenya take steps to ensure that the appropriate use condition is met ahead of the first exchanges of information.

The domestic legal and administrative framework

Kenya does not yet have legislation in place to implement the BEPS Action 13 minimum standard.

It is recommended that Kenya take steps to implement a domestic legal and administrative framework to impose and enforce CbC reporting requirements as soon as possible. This recommendation remains in place since the 2017/2018 peer review.

The exchange of information framework

Kenya has no bilateral relationships in place for the exchange of CbC reports nor processes to ensure that the exchange of information is conducted in a manner consistent with the terms of reference relating to the exchange of information framework.

It is recommended that Kenya take steps to have qualifying competent authority agreements in effect with jurisdictions of the Inclusive Framework that meet the confidentiality, consistency and appropriate use conditions and with which Kenya has an international exchange of information agreement in effect that allows for the automatic exchange of tax information. This recommendation remains in place since the 2017/2018 peer review.

It is recommended that Kenya take steps to implement the necessary processes or written procedures to ensure that the exchange of information is conducted in a manner consistent with the terms of reference relating to the exchange of information framework. This recommendation remains in place since the 2018/2019 peer review.

Appropriate use of CbC reports

Kenya does not yet have controls in place to ensure the appropriate use of CbC reports.

It is recommended that Kenya take steps to ensure that the appropriate use condition is met ahead of the first exchanges of information. This recommendation remains in place since the 2017/2018 peer review.

Korea

Overview of CbC reporting requirements

First reporting fiscal year: Commencing on or after 1 January 2016

Consolidated group revenue threshold: KRW 1 trillion

Filing deadline: 12 months following the end of the reporting fiscal year

Local filing required: Yes

Surrogate parent entity filing permitted: Yes

First review of the domestic legal framework: 2017/2018

Summary of recommendations

Area of implementation	Recommendations for improvement
Domestic legal and administrative framework	None.
Exchange of information framework	None.
Appropriate use	None.

The domestic legal and administrative framework

Korea confirms that its rules have not changed and continue to be applied effectively. Korea continues to meet all terms of reference.

The exchange of information framework

Korea confirms that its rules have not changed and continue to be applied effectively. Korea continues to meet all terms of reference.

Appropriate use of CbC reports

Korea confirms that its rules have not changed and continue to be applied effectively. Korea continues to meet all terms of reference.

Latvia

Overview of CbC reporting requirements

First reporting fiscal year: Commencing on or after 1 January 2016

Consolidated group revenue threshold: EUR 750 million

Filing deadline: 12 months following the end of the reporting fiscal year

Local filing required: Yes

Surrogate parent entity filing permitted: Yes

First review of the domestic legal framework: 2017/2018

Summary of recommendations

Area of implementation	Recommendations for improvement
Domestic legal and administrative framework	None.
Exchange of information framework	None.
Appropriate use	None.

The domestic legal and administrative framework

Latvia's 2017/2018 peer review recommended that Latvia amend or otherwise clarify that the annual consolidated group revenue threshold calculation rule applies in a manner consistent with the OECD guidance on currency fluctuations in respect of an MNE Group whose Ultimate Parent Entity is located in a jurisdiction other than Latvia. A clarification has been issued[1] and this recommendation is therefore removed.[2]

Latvia's domestic legal and administrative framework meets all the terms of reference

The exchange of information framework

Latvia confirms that its rules have not changed and continue to be applied effectively. Latvia continues to meet all terms of reference.

Appropriate use of CbC reports

Latvia confirms that its rules have not changed and continue to be applied effectively. Latvia continues to meet all terms of reference.

Notes

[1] https://www.vid.gov.lv/lv/starptautiskie-ligumi-un-administrativa-sadarbiba.

[2] Latvia's 2017/2018 peer review included a monitoring point relating to the interpretation of the definitions of "Revenues – Related Party". This monitoring point remains in place.

Liberia

Overview of CbC reporting requirements

Liberia has not yet introduced a requirement for the filing of CbC reports, as required under the BEPS Action 13 (CbC reporting) minimum standard.

Summary of recommendations

Area of implementation	Recommendations for improvement
Domestic legal and administrative framework	It is recommended that Liberia take steps to implement a domestic legal and administrative framework to impose and enforce CbC reporting requirements as soon as possible.
Exchange of information framework	It is recommended that Liberia take steps to have qualifying competent authority agreements in effect with jurisdictions of the Inclusive Framework that meet the confidentiality, consistency and appropriate use conditions and with which Liberia has an international exchange of information agreement in effect that allows for the automatic exchange of tax information. It is recommended that Liberia take steps to implement the necessary processes or written procedures to ensure that the exchange of information is conducted in a manner consistent with the terms of reference relating to the exchange of information framework.
Appropriate use	It is recommended that Liberia take steps to ensure that the appropriate use condition is met ahead of the first exchanges of information.

The domestic legal and administrative framework

Liberia does not yet have legislation in place to implement the BEPS Action 13 minimum standard.

It is recommended that Liberia take steps to implement a domestic legal and administrative framework to impose and enforce CbC reporting requirements as soon as possible. This recommendation remains in place since the 2018/2019 peer review.

The exchange of information framework

Liberia has no bilateral relationships in place for the exchange of CbC reports nor processes to ensure that the exchange of information is conducted in a manner consistent with the terms of reference relating to the exchange of information framework.

It is recommended that Liberia take steps to have qualifying competent authority agreements in effect with jurisdictions of the Inclusive Framework that meet the confidentiality, consistency and appropriate use conditions and with which Liberia has an international exchange of information agreement in effect that allows for the automatic exchange of tax information. This recommendation remains in place since the 2018/2019 peer review.

It is recommended that Liberia take steps to implement the necessary processes or written procedures to ensure that the exchange of information is conducted in a manner consistent with the terms of reference relating to the exchange of information framework. This recommendation remains in place since the 2018/2019 peer review.

Appropriate use of CbC reports

Liberia does not yet have controls in place to ensure the appropriate use of CbC reports.

It is recommended that Liberia take steps to ensure that the appropriate use condition is met ahead of the first exchanges of information. This recommendation remains in place since the 2018/2019 peer review.

Liechtenstein

Overview of CbC reporting requirements

First reporting fiscal year: Commencing on or after 1 January 2017. Liechtenstein also allowed MNE Groups to file a CbC report on a voluntary basis, for reporting fiscal years commencing between 1 January 2016 and 31 December 2016.

Consolidated group revenue threshold: CHF 900 million

Filing deadline: 12 months following the end of the reporting fiscal year

Local filing required: Yes

Surrogate parent entity filing permitted: Yes

First review of the domestic legal framework: 2017/2018

Summary of recommendations

Area of implementation	Recommendations for improvement
Domestic legal and administrative framework	None.
Exchange of information framework	None.
Appropriate use	None.

The domestic legal and administrative framework

Liechtenstein confirms that its rules have not changed and continue to be applied effectively. Liechtenstein continues to meet all terms of reference.[1]

The exchange of information framework

Liechtenstein made some exchanges of CbC reports after the deadline. This was caused by a technical fault which has since been resolved and so no recommendation is required.

Liechtenstein confirms that its rules have not changed and continue to be applied effectively. Liechtenstein continues to meet all terms of reference.

Appropriate use of CbC reports

Liechtenstein confirms that its rules have not changed and continue to be applied effectively. Liechtenstein continues to meet all terms of reference.

Note

[1] Liechtenstein's 2017/2018 peer review included a general monitoring point to ensure that legislation setting out local filing requirements is not interpreted as applying to situations where there is no current international agreement between Liechtenstein and the residence jurisdiction of the Ultimate Parent Entity (which is not permitted under the terms of reference).This monitoring point remains in place.

Lithuania

Overview of CbC reporting requirements

First reporting fiscal year: Commencing on or after 1 January 2016

Consolidated group revenue threshold: EUR 750 million

Filing deadline: 12 months following the end of the reporting fiscal year

Local filing required: Yes

Surrogate parent entity filing permitted: Yes

First review of the domestic legal framework: 2017/2018

Summary of recommendations

Area of implementation	Recommendations for improvement
Domestic legal and administrative framework	None.
Exchange of information framework	None.
Appropriate use	None.

The domestic legal and administrative framework

Lithuania confirms that its rules have not changed and continue to be applied effectively. Lithuania continues to meet all terms of reference.[1] [2]

The exchange of information framework

Lithuania confirms that its rules have not changed and continue to be applied effectively. Lithuania continues to meet all terms of reference.

Appropriate use of CbC reports

Lithuania confirms that its rules have not changed and continue to be applied effectively. Lithuania continues to meet all terms of reference.

Notes

[1] Lithuania's 2017/2018 peer review included a monitoring point relating to the definition of "International Corporation Group". This monitoring point remains in place.

[2] Lithuania's 2017/2018 peer review included a monitoring point relating to the interpretation of the definitions of "Revenues – Related Party". This monitoring point remains in place.

Luxembourg

Overview of CbC reporting requirements

First reporting fiscal year: Commencing on or after 1 January 2016

Consolidated group revenue threshold: EUR 750 million

Filing deadline: 12 months following the end of the reporting fiscal year

Local filing required: Yes

Surrogate parent entity filing permitted: Yes

First review of the domestic legal framework: 2017/2018

Summary of recommendations

Area of implementation	Recommendations for improvement
Domestic legal and administrative framework	None.
Exchange of information framework	None.
Appropriate use	None.

The domestic legal and administrative framework

Luxembourg confirms that its rules have not changed and continue to be applied effectively. Luxembourg continues to meet all terms of reference.

The exchange of information framework

Luxembourg confirms that its rules have not changed and continue to be applied effectively. Luxembourg continues to meet all terms of reference.

Appropriate use of CbC reports

Luxembourg confirms that its rules have not changed and continue to be applied effectively. Luxembourg continues to meet all terms of reference.

Macau (China)

Overview of CbC reporting requirements

First reporting fiscal year: Commencing on or after 1 January 2019

Consolidated group revenue threshold: MOP 7 billion

Filing deadline: 12 months following the end of the reporting fiscal year

Local filing required: No

Surrogate parent entity filing permitted: No

First review of the domestic legal framework: 2019/2020

Summary of recommendations

Area of implementation	Recommendations for improvement
Domestic legal and administrative framework	None.
Exchange of information framework	None.
Appropriate use	Not reviewed.

The domestic legal and administrative framework

Macau confirms that its rules have not changed and continue to be applied effectively. Macau continues to meet all terms of reference.

The exchange of information framework

Macau confirms that its rules have not changed and continue to be applied effectively. Macau continues to meet all terms of reference.

Appropriate use of CbC reports

Macau has notified as a non-reciprocal jurisdiction and, as such, will not receive CbC reports submitted to tax authorities in other jurisdictions, and will not apply local filing. It is therefore not necessary for this peer review evaluation to reach any conclusions with respect to Macau's compliance with the terms of reference on appropriate use.

Malaysia

Overview of CbC reporting requirements

First reporting fiscal year: Commencing on or after 1 January 2017. Malaysia also allowed MNE Groups to file a CbC report on a voluntary basis, for reporting fiscal years commencing between 1 January 2016 and 31 December 2016.

Consolidated group revenue threshold: MYR 3 billion

Filing deadline: 12 months following the end of the reporting fiscal year

Local filing required: No

Surrogate parent entity filing permitted: Yes

First review of the domestic legal framework: 2017/2018

Summary of recommendations

Area of implementation	Recommendations for improvement
Domestic legal and administrative framework	None.
Exchange of information framework	None.
Appropriate use	None.

The domestic legal and administrative framework

Malaysia confirms that its rules have not changed and continue to be applied effectively. Malaysia continues to meet all terms of reference.

The exchange of information framework

Malaysia made some exchanges of CbC reports after the deadline. This was caused by a fault in an automated system for exchange which has since been resolved and so no recommendation is required.

Malaysia confirms that its rules have not changed and continue to be applied effectively. Malaysia continues to meet all terms of reference.

Appropriate use of CbC reports

Malaysia confirms that its rules have not changed and continue to be applied effectively. Malaysia continues to meet all terms of reference.

Maldives

Overview of CbC reporting requirements

First reporting fiscal year: Commencing on or after 1 January 2021

Consolidated group revenue threshold: EUR 750 million

Filing deadline: 12 months following the end of the reporting fiscal year

Local filing required: Requirement suspended

Surrogate parent entity filing permitted: Yes

First review of the domestic legal framework: 2020/2021

Summary of recommendations

Area of implementation	Recommendations for improvement
Domestic legal and administrative framework	None.
Exchange of information framework	It is recommended that Maldives take steps to implement the necessary processes or written procedures to ensure that the exchange of information is conducted in a manner consistent with the terms of reference relating to the exchange of information framework.
Appropriate use	A review of Maldives appropriate use controls will be included in the next peer review report.

The domestic legal and administrative framework

Maldives' 2020/2021 peer review recommended that Maldives take steps to amend its legislation or otherwise ensure that local filing requirements only apply in accordance with the terms of reference. Maldives has suspended its local filing requirement until further notice and this recommendation is removed.[1]

Maldives' 2020/2021 peer review included a recommendation that Maldives should clarify that the annual consolidated group revenue threshold calculation rule applies in line with the OECD guidance on currency fluctuations in respect of an MNE Group whose Ultimate Parent Entity is located in a jurisdiction other than Maldives. Maldives has since amended its legislation to reflect this change and this recommendation is therefore removed.[2]

Maldives's domestic legal and administrative framework meets all other terms of reference.

The exchange of information framework

Maldives' 2017/2018 peer review included a recommendation that Maldives take steps to have qualifying competent authority agreements in effect with jurisdictions of the Inclusive Framework that meet the confidentiality, consistency and appropriate use conditions and with which it has an international exchange of information agreement in effect that allows for the automatic exchange of tax information. Maldives has now activated relationships under the Multilateral Competent Authority Agreement for exchanging CbC reports and this recommendation is removed.

It is recommended that Maldives take steps to implement the necessary processes or written procedures to ensure that the exchange of information is conducted in a manner consistent with the terms of reference relating to the exchange of information framework. This recommendation remains in place since the 2018/2019 peer review.

Appropriate use of CbC reports

Maldives' 2017/2018 peer report recommended that steps be taken to ensure that the appropriate use condition is met ahead of the first exchanges of information.

During the peer review, Maldives submitted a notification under the CbC Multilateral Competent Authority Agreement that it is a non-reciprocal jurisdiction for CbC reporting purposes. Shortly before the end of the peer review, Maldives submitted a further notification under the CbC Multilateral Competent Authority Agreement that it is once again a reciprocal jurisdiction. As such, Maldives is now required to ensure that the appropriate use condition is met ahead of its first exchanges of information. It has not been possible to carry out a review of the controls in place to ensure the appropriate use of CbC reports and a review of these processes will take place in the next peer review.

Notes

[1] https://www.mira.gov.mv/TaxLegislation/country-by-country-reporting-regulation-consolidated-english_20220605.pdf.

[2] https://www.mira.gov.mv/TaxLegislation/country-by-country-reporting-regulation-english.pdf.

Malta

Overview of CbC reporting requirements

First reporting fiscal year: Commencing on or after 1 January 2016

Consolidated group revenue threshold: EUR 750 million

Filing deadline: 12 months following the end of the reporting fiscal year

Local filing required: Yes, for reporting fiscal years commencing on or after 1 January 2017

Surrogate parent entity filing permitted: Yes

First review of the domestic legal framework: 2017/2018

Summary of recommendations

Area of implementation	Recommendations for improvement
Domestic legal and administrative framework	None.
Exchange of information framework	None.
Appropriate use	None.

The domestic legal and administrative framework

Malta confirms that its rules have not changed and continue to be applied effectively. Malta continues to meet all terms of reference.

The exchange of information framework

Malta confirms that its rules have not changed and continue to be applied effectively. Malta continues to meet all terms of reference.

Appropriate use of CbC reports

Malta confirms that its rules have not changed and continue to be applied effectively. Malta continues to meet all terms of reference.

Mauritius

Overview of CbC reporting requirements

First reporting fiscal year: Commencing on or after 1 July 2018.

Consolidated group revenue threshold: EUR 750 million

Filing deadline: 12 months following the end of the reporting fiscal year

Local filing required: No

Surrogate parent entity filing permitted: Yes

First review of the domestic legal framework: 2018/2019

Summary of recommendations

Area of implementation	Recommendations for improvement
Domestic legal and administrative framework	None.
Exchange of information framework	None.
Appropriate use	None.

The domestic legal and administrative framework

Mauritius confirms that its rules have not changed and continue to be applied effectively. Mauritius continues to meet all terms of reference.

The exchange of information framework

Mauritius confirms that its rules have not changed and continue to be applied effectively. Mauritius continues to meet all terms of reference.

Appropriate use of CbC reports

Mauritius confirms that its rules have not changed and continue to be applied effectively. Mauritius continues to meet all terms of reference.

Mexico

Overview of CbC reporting requirements

First reporting fiscal year: Commencing on or after 1 January 2016

Consolidated group revenue threshold: MXN 12 billion

Filing deadline: 12 months following the end of the reporting fiscal year

Local filing required: Yes

Surrogate parent entity filing permitted: Yes

First review of the domestic legal framework: 2017/2018

Summary of recommendations

Area of implementation	Recommendations for improvement
Domestic legal and administrative framework	None.
Exchange of information framework	None.
Appropriate use	None.

The domestic legal and administrative framework

Mexico confirms that its rules have not changed and continue to be applied effectively. Mexico continues to meet all terms of reference.[1] [2] [3]

The exchange of information framework

Mexico confirms that its rules have not changed and continue to be applied effectively. Mexico continues to meet all terms of reference.

Appropriate use of CbC reports

Mexico confirms that its rules have not changed and continue to be applied effectively. Mexico continues to meet all terms of reference.

Notes

[1] Mexico's 2017/2018 peer review included a general monitoring point with respect to the annual consolidated group revenue threshold under article 76-A, paragraph III.c.6. of the Mexican Income Tax Law, which may be inconsistent with paragraph 8 a) ii. of the terms of reference, as it may generate fluctuations from year to year on the threshold to require the filing of CbC reports. Mexico indicates that the sole purpose of this provision is to have a legal vehicle in order to change the threshold if such change arises from the 2020 revision. Mexico confirms that there were no yearly fluctuations to the annual consolidated group revenue threshold under article 76-A during the year in review. This monitoring point remains in place.

[2] Mexico's 2017/2018 peer review included a monitoring point relating to the definition of "number of employees" in its legislation. The definition in Mexico's legislation does not mirror the Action 13 Report's specific instructions by not providing flexibility to taxpayers to report independent contractors as employees. However, this does not seem to raise any significant concern, taking into account the particular domestic context as described by Mexico. Mexico confirms that the definition of "number of employees" remains as established since it is intended to address specific issues related to certain tax planning setups relevant in the Mexican context. This monitoring point remains in place.

[3] Mexico's 2017/2018 peer review included a general monitoring point relating to processes that would allow Mexico to take appropriate measures in case it is notified by another jurisdiction that such other jurisdiction has reason to believe that an error may have led to incorrect or incomplete information reporting by a Reporting Entity or that there is non-compliance of a Reporting Entity with respect to its obligation to file a CbC report. This monitoring point remains in place.

Monaco

Overview of CbC reporting requirements

First reporting fiscal year: Commencing on or after 1 January 2018

Consolidated group revenue threshold: EUR 750 million

Filing deadline: 12 months following the end of the reporting fiscal year

Local filing required: No

Surrogate parent entity filing permitted: Yes

First review of the domestic legal framework: 2017/2018

Summary of recommendations

Area of implementation	Recommendations for improvement
Domestic legal and administrative framework	None.
Exchange of information framework	None.
Appropriate use	None.

The domestic legal and administrative framework

Monaco confirms that its rules have not changed and continue to be applied effectively. Monaco continues to meet all terms of reference.

The exchange of information framework

Monaco's 2018/2019 peer report included a recommendation that Monaco take steps to implement processes or written procedures to ensure that the exchange of information is conducted in a manner consistent with the terms of reference relating to the exchange of information framework. Further information has been received showing that these processes are in place and this recommendation is therefore removed.

Appropriate use of CbC reports

Monaco confirms that its rules have not changed and continue to be applied effectively. Monaco continues to meet all terms of reference.

Mongolia

Overview of CbC reporting requirements

First reporting fiscal year: Commencing on or after 1 January 2020

Consolidated group revenue threshold: MNT1.7 trillion

Filing deadline: 12 months following the end of the reporting fiscal year

Local filing required: Yes

Surrogate parent entity filing permitted: Yes

First review of the domestic legal framework: 2020/2021

Summary of recommendations

Area of implementation	Recommendations for improvement
Domestic legal and administrative framework	It is recommended that Mongolia take steps to ensure that local filing only occurs in the circumstances permitted under the minimum standard. It is recommended that Mongolia clarify that the annual consolidated group revenue threshold calculation rule applies in line with the OECD guidance on currency fluctuations in respect of an MNE Group whose Ultimate Parent Entity is located in a jurisdiction other than Mongolia.
Exchange of information framework	It is recommended that Mongolia take steps to have qualifying competent authority agreements in effect with jurisdictions of the Inclusive Framework that meet the confidentiality, consistency and appropriate use conditions and with which Mongolia has an international exchange of information agreement in effect that allows for the automatic exchange of tax information. It is recommended that Mongolia take steps to implement the necessary processes or written procedures to ensure that the exchange of information is conducted in a manner consistent with the terms of reference relating to the exchange of information framework.
Appropriate use	It is recommended that Mongolia take steps to ensure that the appropriate use condition is met ahead of the first exchanges of information.

The domestic legal and administrative framework

It is recommended that Mongolia amend its legislation or otherwise take steps to ensure that provisions to enforce the effective implementation of CbC reporting requirements are provided for. This recommendation remains in place since the 2020/2021 peer review.

It is recommended that Mongolia take steps to amend its legislation or otherwise alter the threshold condition to bring it in line with the Action 13 minimum standard. This recommendation remains in place since the 2020/2021 peer review.

Mongolia's domestic legal and administrative framework meets all other terms of reference.

The exchange of information framework

Mongolia has no bilateral relationships in place for the exchange of CbC reports nor processes to ensure that the exchange of information is conducted in a manner consistent with the terms of reference relating to the exchange of information framework.

It is recommended that Mongolia take steps to have qualifying competent authority agreements in effect with jurisdictions of the Inclusive Framework that meet the confidentiality, consistency and appropriate use conditions and with which Mongolia has an international exchange of information agreement in effect that allows for the automatic exchange of tax information. This recommendation remains in place since the 2018/2019 peer review.

It is recommended that Mongolia take steps to implement the necessary processes or written procedures to ensure that the exchange of information is conducted in a manner consistent with the terms of reference relating to the exchange of information framework. This recommendation remains in place since the 2018/2019 peer review.

Appropriate use of CbC reports

Mongolia does not yet have controls in place to ensure the appropriate use of CbC reports.

It is recommended that Mongolia take steps to ensure that the appropriate use condition is met ahead of the first exchanges of information. This recommendation remains in place since the 2018/2019 peer review.

Montenegro

Overview of CbC reporting requirements

Montenegro has implemented a domestic legal and administrative framework for CbC reporting and a review of this will be included in the next peer review report.

Summary of recommendations

Area of implementation	Recommendations for improvement
Domestic legal and administrative framework	A review of Montenegro's domestic legal and administrative framework will be undertaken as part of the next BEPS Action 13 peer review.
Exchange of information framework	It is recommended that Montenegro take steps to have qualifying competent authority agreements in effect with jurisdictions of the Inclusive Framework that meet the confidentiality, consistency and appropriate use conditions and with which Montenegro has an international exchange of information agreement in effect that allows for the automatic exchange of tax information. It is recommended that Montenegro take steps to implement the necessary processes or written procedures to ensure that the exchange of information is conducted in a manner consistent with the terms of reference relating to the exchange of information framework.
Appropriate use	It is recommended that Montenegro take steps to ensure that the appropriate use condition is met ahead of the first exchanges of information.

The domestic legal and administrative framework

Montenegro has introduced a CbC reporting filing requirement, as required under the BEPS Action 13 (CbC reporting) minimum standard. It has not been possible to carry out a review of this legislation for this peer review. The recommendation for Montenegro to implement legislation is therefore removed and review of the legislation will take place next year.

The exchange of information framework

Montenegro has no bilateral relationships in place for the exchange of CbC reports nor processes to ensure that the exchange of information is conducted in a manner consistent with the terms of reference relating to the exchange of information framework.

It is recommended that Montenegro take steps to have qualifying competent authority agreements in effect with jurisdictions of the Inclusive Framework that meet the confidentiality, consistency and appropriate use conditions and with which Montenegro has an international exchange of information agreement in effect that allows for the automatic exchange of tax information.

It is recommended that Montenegro take steps to implement the necessary processes or written procedures to ensure that the exchange of information is conducted in a manner consistent with the terms of reference relating to the exchange of information framework.

Appropriate use of CbC reports

Montenegro does not yet have controls in place to ensure the appropriate use of CbC reports.

It is recommended that Montenegro take steps to ensure that the appropriate use condition is met ahead of the first exchanges of information.

Montserrat

Overview of CbC reporting requirements

Montserrat has not yet introduced a requirement for the filing of CbC reports, as required under the BEPS Action 13 (CbC reporting) minimum standard.

Summary of recommendations

Area of implementation	Recommendations for improvement
Domestic legal and administrative framework	It is recommended that Montserrat take steps to implement a domestic legal and administrative framework to impose and enforce CbC reporting requirements as soon as possible.
Exchange of information framework	It is recommended that Montserrat take steps to have qualifying competent authority agreements in effect with jurisdictions of the Inclusive Framework that meet the confidentiality, consistency and appropriate use conditions and with which Montserrat has an international exchange of information agreement in effect that allows for the automatic exchange of tax information. It is recommended that Montserrat take steps to implement the necessary processes or written procedures to ensure that the exchange of information is conducted in a manner consistent with the terms of reference relating to the exchange of information framework.
Appropriate use	It is recommended that Montserrat take steps to ensure that the appropriate use condition is met ahead of the first exchanges of information.

The domestic legal and administrative framework

Montserrat does not yet have legislation in place to implement the BEPS Action 13 minimum standard.

It is recommended that Montserrat take steps to implement a domestic legal and administrative framework to impose and enforce CbC reporting requirements as soon as possible. This recommendation remains in place since the 2018/2019 peer review.

The exchange of information framework

Montserrat has no bilateral relationships in place for the exchange of CbC reports nor processes to ensure that the exchange of information is conducted in a manner consistent with the terms of reference relating to the exchange of information framework.

It is recommended that Montserrat take steps to have qualifying competent authority agreements in effect with jurisdictions of the Inclusive Framework that meet the confidentiality, consistency and appropriate use conditions and with which Montserrat has an international exchange of information agreement in effect that allows for the automatic exchange of tax information. This recommendation remains in place since the 2018/2019 peer review.

It is recommended that Montserrat take steps to implement the necessary processes or written procedures to ensure that the exchange of information is conducted in a manner consistent with the terms of reference relating to the exchange of information framework. This recommendation remains in place since the 2018/2019 peer review.

Appropriate use of CbC reports

Montserrat does not yet have controls in place to ensure the appropriate use of CbC reports.

It is recommended that Montserrat take steps to ensure that the appropriate use condition is met ahead of the first exchanges of information. This recommendation remains in place since the 2018/2019 peer review.

Morocco

Overview of CbC reporting requirements

First reporting fiscal year: Commencing on or after 1 January 2021

Consolidated group revenue threshold: MAD 8,122,500 thousand

Filing deadline: 12 months following the end of the reporting fiscal year

Local filing required: Yes

Surrogate parent entity filing permitted: Yes

First review of the domestic legal framework: 2020/2021

Summary of recommendations

Area of implementation	Recommendations for improvement
Domestic legal and administrative framework	It is recommended that Morocco take steps to ensure that local filing only occurs in the circumstances permitted under the minimum standard. It is recommended that Morocco clarify that the annual consolidated group revenue threshold calculation rule applies in line with the OECD guidance on currency fluctuations in respect of an MNE Group whose Ultimate Parent Entity is located in a jurisdiction other than Morocco.
Exchange of information framework	It is recommended that Morocco take steps to have qualifying competent authority agreements in effect with jurisdictions of the Inclusive Framework that meet the confidentiality, consistency and appropriate use conditions and with which Morocco has an international exchange of information agreement in effect that allows for the automatic exchange of tax information. It is recommended that Morocco take steps to implement processes or written procedures to ensure that the exchange of information is conducted in a manner consistent with the terms of reference relating to the exchange of information framework ahead of the first exchanges of information.
Appropriate use	It is recommended that Morocco take steps to ensure that the appropriate use condition is met ahead of the first exchanges of information.

The domestic legal and administrative framework

Morocco has a legislative requirement for local filing which is in effect despite Morocco not yet meeting all of the consistency, confidentiality and appropriate use conditions. It is therefore recommended that Morocco take steps to ensure that local filing only occurs in the circumstances permitted under the minimum standard. This recommendation remains in place since the 2020/2021 peer review.

It is recommended that Morocco clarify that the annual consolidated group revenue threshold calculation rule applies in line with the OECD guidance on currency fluctuations in respect of an MNE Group whose Ultimate Parent Entity is located in a jurisdiction other than Morocco. This recommendation remains in place since the 2020/2021 peer review.

Morocco's domestic legal and administrative framework meets all other terms of reference.

The exchange of information framework

Morocco has no bilateral relationships in place for the exchange of CbC reports nor processes to ensure that the exchange of information is conducted in a manner consistent with the terms of reference relating to the exchange of information framework.

It is recommended that Morocco take steps to have qualifying competent authority agreements in effect with jurisdictions of the Inclusive Framework that meet the confidentiality, consistency and appropriate use conditions and with which Morocco has an international exchange of information agreement in effect that allows for the automatic exchange of tax information. This recommendation remains in place since the 2019/2020 peer review.

It is recommended that Morocco take steps to implement processes or written procedures to ensure that the exchange of information is conducted in a manner consistent with the terms of reference relating to the exchange of information framework ahead of the first exchanges of information. This recommendation remains in place since the 2019/2020 peer review.

Appropriate use of CbC reports

Morocco does not yet have controls in place to ensure the appropriate use of CbC reports.

It is recommended that Morocco take steps to ensure that the appropriate use condition is met ahead of the first exchanges of information. This recommendation remains in place since the 2019/2020 peer review.

Namibia

Overview of CbC reporting requirements

Namibia has not yet introduced a requirement for the filing of CbC reports, as required under the BEPS Action 13 (CbC reporting) minimum standard.

Summary of recommendations

Area of implementation	Recommendations for improvement
Domestic legal and administrative framework	It is recommended that Namibia take steps to implement a domestic legal and administrative framework to impose and enforce CbC reporting requirements as soon as possible.
Exchange of information framework	It is recommended that Namibia take steps to have qualifying competent authority agreements in effect with jurisdictions of the Inclusive Framework that meet the confidentiality, consistency and appropriate use conditions and with which Namibia has an international exchange of information agreement in effect that allows for the automatic exchange of tax information. It is recommended that Namibia take steps to implement the necessary processes or written procedures to ensure that the exchange of information is conducted in a manner consistent with the terms of reference relating to the exchange of information framework.
Appropriate use	It is recommended that Namibia take steps to ensure that the appropriate use condition is met ahead of the first exchanges of information.

The domestic legal and administrative framework

Namibia does not yet have legislation in place to implement the BEPS Action 13 minimum standard.

It is recommended that Namibia take steps to implement a domestic legal and administrative framework to impose and enforce CbC reporting requirements as soon as possible. This recommendation remains in place since the 2019/2020 peer review.

The exchange of information framework

Namibia has no bilateral relationships in place for the exchange of CbC reports nor processes to ensure that the exchange of information is conducted in a manner consistent with the terms of reference relating to the exchange of information framework.

It is recommended that Namibia take steps to have qualifying competent authority agreements in effect with jurisdictions of the Inclusive Framework that meet the confidentiality, consistency and appropriate use conditions and with which Namibia has an international exchange of information agreement in effect that allows for the automatic exchange of tax information. This recommendation remains in place since the 2019/2020 peer review.

It is recommended that Namibia take steps to implement the necessary processes or written procedures to ensure that the exchange of information is conducted in a manner consistent with the terms of reference relating to the exchange of information framework. This recommendation remains in place since the 2019/2020 peer review.

Appropriate use of CbC reports

Namibia does not yet have controls in place to ensure the appropriate use of CbC reports.

It is recommended that Namibia take steps to ensure that the appropriate use condition is met ahead of the first exchanges of information. This recommendation remains in place since the 2019/2020 peer review.

Netherlands

Overview of CbC reporting requirements

First reporting fiscal year: Commencing on or after 1 January 2016

Consolidated group revenue threshold: EUR 750 million

Filing deadline: 12 months following the end of the reporting fiscal year

Local filing required: Yes

Surrogate parent entity filing permitted: Yes

First review of the domestic legal framework: 2017/2018

Summary of recommendations

Area of implementation	Recommendations for improvement
Domestic legal and administrative framework	None.
Exchange of information framework	None.
Appropriate use	None.

The domestic legal and administrative framework

The Netherlands confirms that its rules have not changed and continue to be applied effectively. The Netherlands continues to meet all terms of reference.

The exchange of information framework

The Netherlands confirms that its rules have not changed and continue to be applied effectively. The Netherlands continues to meet all terms of reference.

Appropriate use of CbC reports

The Netherlands confirms that its rules have not changed and continue to be applied effectively. The Netherlands continues to meet all terms of reference.

New Zealand

Overview of CbC reporting requirements

First reporting fiscal year: Commencing on or after 1 January 2016

Consolidated group revenue threshold: EUR 750 million

Filing deadline: 12 months following the end of the reporting fiscal year

Local filing required: No

Surrogate parent entity filing permitted: Yes

First review of the domestic legal framework: 2017/2018

Summary of recommendations

Area of implementation	Recommendations for improvement
Domestic legal and administrative framework	None.
Exchange of information framework	None.
Appropriate use	None.

The domestic legal and administrative framework

New Zealand confirms that its rules have not changed and continue to be applied effectively. New Zealand continues to meet all terms of reference.[1] [2] [3]

The exchange of information framework

New Zealand confirms that its rules have not changed and continue to be applied effectively. New Zealand continues to meet all terms of reference.

Appropriate use of CbC reports

New Zealand confirms that its rules have not changed and continue to be applied effectively. New Zealand continues to meet all terms of reference.

Notes

[1] New Zealand's 2017/2018 peer review included a monitoring point referring to the definition of a "large multinational group" in its legislation does which not include the "deemed listing provision" as required under the terms of reference. However, New Zealand notes that the financial reporting requirements in New Zealand apply to large entities (including companies, partnerships and limited partnerships) regardless of whether they are listed on a stock exchange. A "large entity" is defined in the Financial Reporting Act 2013 as an entity that earns over NZD 30m of consolidated revenues (which is much lower than EUR 750m) or that have over NZD 60m of consolidated assets in the previous two years. New Zealand also confirms that in the very unlikely event that an entity did not prepare consolidated financial statements and would be considered as an "Ultimate Parent Entity" further to the "deemed listing provision" (as per paragraph 18.i. of the terms of reference), the existing powers of Section 17 of the Tax Administration Act 1994 will be relied on to request the information. This monitoring point remains in place.

[2] As New Zealand continues to rely on existing powers in the Tax Administration Act 1994 until legislation is finalised, and because the effectiveness of this system still relies on the fact that the Inland Revenue correctly identifies all New Zealand resident entities that are the Ultimate Parent Entity of an MNE Group within the scope of CbC Reporting and issues a notification, the monitoring point in the 2017/2018 peer review relating to New Zealand's framework remains in place.

[3] New Zealand's 2017/2018 peer review included a general monitoring point relating to a specific process that would allow New Zealand to take appropriate measures in case New Zealand is notified by another jurisdiction that such other jurisdiction has reason to believe that an error may have led to incorrect or incomplete information reporting by a Reporting Entity or that there is non-compliance of a Reporting Entity with respect to its obligation to file a CbC report. This monitoring point remains in place.

Nigeria

Overview of CbC reporting requirements

First reporting fiscal year: Commencing on or after 1 January 2018

Consolidated group revenue threshold: NGN 160 billion

Filing deadline: 12 months following the end of the reporting fiscal year

Local filing required: Requirement suspended

Surrogate parent entity filing permitted: Yes

First review of the domestic legal framework: 2017/2018

Summary of recommendations

Area of implementation	Recommendations for improvement
Domestic legal and administrative framework	None.
Exchange of information framework	It is recommended that Nigeria have in place the necessary processes or written procedures to ensure that the exchange of information is conducted in a manner consistent with the terms of reference relating to the exchange of information framework.
Appropriate use	None.

The domestic legal and administrative framework

Nigeria confirms that its rules have not changed and continue to be applied effectively. Nigeria continues to meet all terms of reference.

The exchange of information framework

Nigeria has notified as a reciprocal jurisdiction but has not yet been able to exchange any CbC reports. It is recommended that Nigeria have in place the necessary processes or written procedures to ensure that the exchange of information is conducted in a manner consistent with the terms of reference relating to the exchange of information framework. This recommendation remains in place since the 2018/2019 peer review.

Appropriate use of CbC reports

Nigeria's 2020/2021 peer report did not reach any conclusions with regard to appropriate use of CbC reports as Nigeria was a non-reciprocal jurisdiction. Nigeria has now notified as a reciprocal jurisdiction.

Before notifying as a non-reciprocal jurisdiction, Nigeria's controls to ensure the appropriate use of CbC reports were reviewed as part of the 2018/2019 peer review and that review concluded that Nigeria met the terms of reference. Nigeria confirms that its rules have not changed since that time and continue to be applied effectively. Nigeria continues to meet all terms of reference.

North Macedonia (Republic of)

Overview of CbC reporting requirements

The Republic of North Macedonia (North Macedonia) has not yet introduced a requirement for the filing of CbC reports, as required under the BEPS Action 13 (CbC reporting) minimum standard.

Summary of recommendations

Area of implementation	Recommendations for improvement
Domestic legal and administrative framework	It is recommended that North Macedonia take steps to implement a domestic legal and administrative framework to impose and enforce CbC reporting requirements as soon as possible.
Exchange of information framework	It is recommended that North Macedonia take steps to have qualifying competent authority agreements in effect with jurisdictions of the Inclusive Framework that meet the confidentiality, consistency and appropriate use conditions and with which North Macedonia has an international exchange of information agreement in effect that allows for the automatic exchange of tax information. It is recommended that North Macedonia take steps to implement the necessary processes or written procedures to ensure that the exchange of information is conducted in a manner consistent with the terms of reference relating to the exchange of information framework.
Appropriate use	It is recommended that North Macedonia take steps to ensure that the appropriate use condition is met ahead of the first exchanges of information.

The domestic legal and administrative framework

North Macedonia does not yet have legislation in place to implement the BEPS Action 13 minimum standard.

It is recommended that North Macedonia take steps to implement a domestic legal and administrative framework to impose and enforce CbC reporting requirements as soon as possible. This recommendation remains in place since the 2018/2019 peer review.

The exchange of information framework

North Macedonia has no bilateral relationships in place for the exchange of CbC reports nor processes to ensure that the exchange of information is conducted in a manner consistent with the terms of reference relating to the exchange of information framework.

It is recommended that North Macedonia take steps to have qualifying competent authority agreements in effect with jurisdictions of the Inclusive Framework that meet the confidentiality, consistency and appropriate use conditions and with which North Macedonia has an international exchange of information agreement in effect that allows for the automatic exchange of tax information. This recommendation remains in place since the 2018/2019 peer review.

It is recommended that North Macedonia take steps to implement the necessary processes or written procedures to ensure that the exchange of information is conducted in a manner consistent with the terms of reference relating to the exchange of information framework. This recommendation remains in place since the 2018/2019 peer review.

Appropriate use of CbC reports

North Macedonia does not yet have controls in place to ensure the appropriate use of CbC reports.

It is recommended that North Macedonia take steps to ensure that the appropriate use condition is met ahead of the first exchanges of information. This recommendation remains in place since the 2018/2019 peer review.

Norway

Overview of CbC reporting requirements

First reporting fiscal year: Commencing on or after 1 January 2016

Consolidated group revenue threshold: NOK 6.5 billion

Filing deadline: 12 months following the end of the reporting fiscal year

Local filing required: Yes

Surrogate parent entity filing permitted: Yes

First review of the domestic legal framework: 2017/2018

Summary of recommendations

Area of implementation	Recommendations for improvement
Domestic legal and administrative framework	None.
Exchange of information framework	None.
Appropriate use	None.

The domestic legal and administrative framework

Norway confirms that its rules have not changed and continue to be applied effectively. Norway continues to meet all terms of reference.[1]

The exchange of information framework

Norway confirms that its rules have not changed and continue to be applied effectively. Norway continues to meet all terms of reference.

Appropriate use of CbC reports

Norway confirms that its rules have not changed and continue to be applied effectively. Norway continues to meet all terms of reference.

Note

[1] Norway's 2017/2018 peer review included a monitoring point relating to the interpretation of the concept of "Systemic Failure". This monitoring point remains in place.

Oman

Overview of CbC reporting requirements

First reporting fiscal year: Commencing on or after 1 January 2020

Consolidated group revenue threshold: OMR 300 million

Filing deadline: 12 months following the end of the reporting fiscal year

Local filing required: Requirement suspended

Surrogate parent entity filing permitted: Yes

First review of the domestic legal framework: 2020/2021

Summary of recommendations

Area of implementation	Recommendations for improvement
Domestic legal and administrative framework	None.
Exchange of information framework	It is recommended that Oman take steps to implement the necessary processes or written procedures to ensure that the exchange of information is conducted in a manner consistent with the terms of reference relating to the exchange of information framework.
Appropriate use	Not reviewed.

The domestic legal and administrative framework

Oman's 2020/2021 peer review recommended that Oman clarify that the annual consolidated group revenue threshold calculation rule applies in line with the OECD guidance on currency fluctuations in respect of an MNE Group whose Ultimate Parent Entity is located in a jurisdiction other than Oman. Oman has issued guidance making this clarification and the recommendation is removed.[1]

Oman's domestic legal and administrative framework meets all the other terms of reference.

The exchange of information framework

It is recommended that Oman take steps to implement the necessary processes or written procedures to ensure that the exchange of information is conducted in a manner consistent with the terms of reference relating to the exchange of information framework. This recommendation remains in place since the 2018/2019 peer review.

Appropriate use of CbC reports

Oman is a non-reciprocal jurisdiction and, as such, will not receive CbC reports submitted to tax authorities in other jurisdictions, and will not apply local filing. It is not necessary for this peer review evaluation to reach any conclusion with respect to Oman's compliance with the terms of reference on appropriate use.

Note

[1] https://www.taxoman.gov.om/portal/documents/20126/2683313/Guidelines+on+the+Country+by+Country+Reporting+%28CbCR%29.pdf/6a575174-19ed-3ea4-46b9-8c40e770c5ac?download=true.

Pakistan

Overview of CbC reporting requirements

First reporting fiscal year: Commencing on or after 1 January 2016

Consolidated group revenue threshold: EUR 750 million

Filing deadline: 12 months following the end of the reporting fiscal year

Local filing required: Yes, for reporting fiscal years commencing on or after 1 January 2017

Surrogate parent entity filing permitted: Yes

First review of the domestic legal framework: 2017/2018

Summary of recommendations

Area of implementation	Recommendations for improvement
Domestic legal and administrative framework	None.
Exchange of information framework	It is recommended that Pakistan take steps to implement processes or written procedures to ensure that the exchange of information is conducted in a manner consistent with the terms of reference relating to the exchange of information framework.
Appropriate use	None.

The domestic legal and administrative framework

Pakistan confirms that its rules have not changed and continue to be applied effectively. Pakistan continues to meet all terms of reference.

The exchange of information framework

It is recommended that Pakistan take steps to implement processes or written procedures to ensure that the exchange of information is conducted in a manner consistent with the terms of reference relating to the exchange of information framework. This recommendation remains in place since the 2018/2019 peer review.

Pakistan's 2020/2021 peer review report included a recommendation to take steps to ensure that timing and accuracy of reports received and exchanged are recorded and available. Pakistan has since taken such steps and this recommendation is therefore removed.

Pakistan notified some late exchanges of CbC reports, due to a technical issue with their portal. This has now been fixed and so no recommendation has been made.

Appropriate use of CbC reports

Pakistan confirms that its rules have not changed and continue to be applied effectively. Pakistan continues to meet all terms of reference.

Panama

Overview of CbC reporting requirements

First reporting fiscal year: Commencing on or after 1 January 2018

Consolidated group revenue threshold: EUR 750 million

Filing deadline: 12 months following the end of the reporting fiscal year

Local filing required: No

Surrogate parent entity filing permitted: Yes

First review of the domestic legal framework: 2019/2020

Summary of recommendations

Area of implementation	Recommendations for improvement
Domestic legal and administrative framework	None.
Exchange of information framework	It is recommended that Panama take steps to implement processes or written procedures to ensure that the exchange of information is conducted in a manner consistent with the terms of reference relating to the exchange of information framework.
Appropriate use	None.

The domestic legal and administrative framework

Panama's 2019/2020 peer review recommended that Panama take steps to implement a penalty regime in order to enforce the timely and accurate filing of CbC reports. A penalty regime has been introduced by Panama and this recommendation is therefore removed.[1]

The exchange of information framework

It is recommended that Panama take steps to implement processes or written procedures to ensure that the exchange of information is conducted in a manner consistent with the terms of reference relating to the exchange of information framework. This recommendation remains in place since the 2018/2019 peer review.

Appropriate use of CbC reports

Panama's 2017/2018 peer review recommended that Panama take steps to ensure that the appropriate use condition is met. Panama has provided details of the controls it has in place to ensure the appropriate use of CbC reports, which comply with published Guidance on the Appropriate Use of Information Contained in CbC Reports.

Note

[1] https://www.gacetaoficial.gob.pa/pdfTemp/29413_A/88359.pdf.

Papua New Guinea

Overview of CbC reporting requirements

First reporting fiscal year: Commencing on or after 1 January 2017

Consolidated group revenue threshold: PGK 2.3 billion

Filing deadline: 12 months following the end of the reporting fiscal year

Local filing required: No

Surrogate parent entity filing permitted: Yes

First review of the domestic legal framework: 2018/2019

Summary of recommendations

Area of implementation	Recommendations for improvement
Domestic legal and administrative framework	It is recommended that Papua New Guinea take steps to amend its legislation or otherwise alter the threshold condition to bring it in line with the Action 13 minimum standard. It is recommended that Papua New Guinea amend its legislation or otherwise take steps to ensure that provisions to enforce the effective implementation of CbC reporting requirements are provided for.
Exchange of information framework	It is recommended that Papua New Guinea take steps to put in place an exchange of information framework that allows automatic exchange of information and have QCAAs in effect with jurisdictions of the Inclusive Framework which meet the confidentiality, consistency and appropriate use prerequisites and with which they have an international exchange of information agreement in effect that allows for the automatic exchange of tax information. It is recommended that Papua New Guinea take steps to implement processes or written procedures to ensure that the exchange of information is conducted in a manner consistent with the terms of reference relating to the exchange of information framework ahead of the first exchanges of information.
Appropriate use	It is recommended that Papua New Guinea take steps to ensure that the appropriate use condition is met ahead of the first exchanges of information.

The domestic legal and administrative framework

It is recommended that Papua New Guinea take steps to amend its legislation or otherwise alter the threshold condition to bring it in line with the Action 13 minimum standard. This recommendation remains in place since the 2018/2019 peer review.

It is recommended that Papua New Guinea amend its legislation or otherwise take steps to ensure that provisions to enforce the effective implementation of CbC reporting requirements are provided for. This recommendation remains in place since the 2018/2019 peer review.

The exchange of information framework

Papua New Guinea has no bilateral relationships in place for the exchange of CbC reports nor processes to ensure that the exchange of information is conducted in a manner consistent with the terms of reference relating to the exchange of information framework.

It is recommended that Papua New Guinea take steps to put in place an exchange of information framework that allows automatic exchange of information and have QCAAs in effect with jurisdictions of the Inclusive Framework which meet the confidentiality, consistency and appropriate use prerequisites and with which they have an international exchange of information agreement in effect that allows for the automatic exchange of tax information. This recommendation remains in place since the 2018/2019 peer review.

It is recommended that Papua New Guinea take steps to implement processes or written procedures to ensure that the exchange of information is conducted in a manner consistent with the terms of reference relating to the exchange of information framework ahead of the first exchanges of information. This recommendation remains in place since the 2018/2019 peer review.

Appropriate use of CbC reports

Papua New Guinea does not yet have controls in place to ensure the appropriate use of CbC reports.

It is recommended that Papua New Guinea take steps to ensure that the appropriate use condition is met ahead of the first exchanges of information. This recommendation remains in place since the 2018/2019 peer review.

Paraguay

Overview of CbC reporting requirements

Paraguay has not yet introduced a requirement for the filing of CbC reports, as required under the BEPS Action 13 (CbC reporting) minimum standard.

Summary of recommendations

Area of implementation	Recommendations for improvement
Domestic legal and administrative framework	It is recommended that Paraguay take steps to implement a domestic legal and administrative framework to impose and enforce CbC reporting requirements as soon as possible.
Exchange of information framework	It is recommended that Paraguay take steps to have qualifying competent authority agreements in effect with jurisdictions of the Inclusive Framework that meet the confidentiality, consistency and appropriate use conditions and with which Paraguay has an international exchange of information agreement in effect that allows for the automatic exchange of tax information. It is recommended that Paraguay take steps to implement the necessary processes or written procedures to ensure that the exchange of information is conducted in a manner consistent with the terms of reference relating to the exchange of information framework.
Appropriate use	It is recommended that Paraguay take steps to ensure that the appropriate use condition is met ahead of the first exchanges of information.

The domestic legal and administrative framework

Paraguay does not yet have legislation in place to implement the BEPS Action 13 minimum standard.

It is recommended that Paraguay take steps to implement a domestic legal and administrative framework to impose and enforce CbC reporting requirements as soon as possible. This recommendation remains in place since the 2017/2018 peer review.

The exchange of information framework

Paraguay has no bilateral relationships in place for the exchange of CbC reports nor processes to ensure that the exchange of information is conducted in a manner consistent with the terms of reference relating to the exchange of information framework.

It is recommended that Paraguay take steps to have qualifying competent authority agreements in effect with jurisdictions of the Inclusive Framework that meet the confidentiality, consistency and appropriate use conditions and with which Paraguay has an international exchange of information agreement in effect that allows for the automatic exchange of tax information. This recommendation remains in place since the 2017/2018 peer review.

It is recommended that Paraguay take steps to implement the necessary processes or written procedures to ensure that the exchange of information is conducted in a manner consistent with the terms of reference relating to the exchange of information framework. This recommendation remains in place since the 2018/2019 peer review.

Appropriate use of CbC reports

Paraguay does not yet have controls in place to ensure the appropriate use of CbC reports.

It is recommended that Paraguay take steps to ensure that the appropriate use condition is met ahead of the first exchanges of information. This recommendation remains in place since the 2017/2018 peer review.

Peru

Overview of CbC reporting requirements

First reporting fiscal year: Commencing on or after 1 January 2017

Consolidated group revenue threshold: PEN 2.7 billion

Filing deadline: 12 months following the end of the reporting fiscal year

Local filing required: Yes

Surrogate parent entity filing permitted: Yes

First review of the domestic legal framework: 2017/2018

Summary of recommendations

Area of implementation	Recommendations for improvement
Domestic legal and administrative framework	None.
Exchange of information framework	None.
Appropriate use	None.

The domestic legal and administrative framework

Peru confirms that its rules have not changed and continue to be applied effectively. Peru continues to meet all terms of reference.

The exchange of information framework

Peru confirms that its rules have not changed and continue to be applied effectively. Peru continues to meet all terms of reference.

Appropriate use of CbC reports

Peru confirms that its rules have not changed and continue to be applied effectively. Peru continues to meet all terms of reference.

Poland

Overview of CbC reporting requirements

First reporting fiscal year: Commencing on or after 1 January 2016

Consolidated group revenue threshold: EUR 750 million

Filing deadline: 12 months following the end of the reporting fiscal year

Local filing required: Yes, for reporting fiscal years commencing on or after 1 January 2017

Surrogate parent entity filing permitted: Yes

First review of the domestic legal framework: 2017/2018

Summary of recommendations

Area of implementation	Recommendations for improvement
Domestic legal and administrative framework	None.
Exchange of information framework	None.
Appropriate use	None.

The domestic legal and administrative framework

Poland confirms that its rules have not changed and continue to be applied effectively. Poland continues to meet all terms of reference.

The exchange of information framework

Poland confirms that its rules have not changed and continue to be applied effectively. Poland continues to meet all terms of reference.

Appropriate use of CbC reports

Poland confirms that its rules have not changed and continue to be applied effectively. Poland continues to meet all terms of reference.

Portugal

Overview of CbC reporting requirements

First reporting fiscal year: Commencing on or after 1 January 2016

Consolidated group revenue threshold: EUR 750 million

Filing deadline: 12 months following the end of the reporting fiscal year

Local filing required: Yes, for reporting fiscal years commencing on or after 1 January 2017

Surrogate parent entity filing permitted: Yes

First review of the domestic legal framework: 2017/2018

Summary of recommendations

Area of implementation	Recommendations for improvement
Domestic legal and administrative framework	None.
Exchange of information framework	None.
Appropriate use	None.

The domestic legal and administrative framework

Portugal confirms that its rules have not changed and continue to be applied effectively. Portugal continues to meet all terms of reference.

The exchange of information framework

Portugal confirms that its rules have not changed and continue to be applied effectively. Portugal continues to meet all terms of reference.

Appropriate use of CbC reports

Portugal confirms that its rules have not changed and continue to be applied effectively. Portugal continues to meet all terms of reference.

Qatar

Overview of CbC reporting requirements

First reporting fiscal year: Commencing on or after 1 January 2018

Consolidated group revenue threshold: QAR 3 billion

Filing deadline: 12 months following the end of the reporting fiscal year

Local filing required: No

Surrogate parent entity filing permitted: Yes

First review of the domestic legal framework: 2017/2018

Summary of recommendations

Area of implementation	Recommendations for improvement
Domestic legal and administrative framework	None.
Exchange of information framework	None.
Appropriate use	Not reviewed.

The domestic legal and administrative framework

Qatar confirms that its rules have not changed and continue to be applied effectively. Qatar continues to meet all terms of reference.[1]

The exchange of information framework

Qatar confirms that its rules have not changed and continue to be applied effectively. Qatar continues to meet all terms of reference.

Appropriate use of CbC reports

Qatar is a non-reciprocal jurisdiction and, as such, will not receive CbC reports submitted to tax authorities in other jurisdictions, and will not apply local filing. It is not necessary for this peer review to reach any conclusion with respect to Qatar's compliance with the terms of reference on appropriate use.

Note

[1] Qatar's 2017/2018 peer review included a monitoring point relating to the definition of "Excluded MNE Group". This monitoring point remains in place.

Romania

Overview of CbC reporting requirements

First reporting fiscal year: Commencing on or after 1 January 2016

Consolidated group revenue threshold: EUR 750 million

Filing deadline: 12 months following the end of the reporting fiscal year

Local filing required: Yes, for reporting fiscal years commencing on or after 1 January 2017

Surrogate parent entity filing permitted: Yes

First review of the domestic legal framework: 2017/2018

Summary of recommendations

Area of implementation	Recommendations for improvement
Domestic legal and administrative framework	It is recommended that Romania take steps amend its legislation or otherwise clarify that local filing is only required in line with the minimum standard for Action 13.
Exchange of information framework	It is recommended that Romania take steps to implement processes or written procedures to ensure that the exchange of information is conducted in a manner consistent with the terms of reference relating to the exchange of information framework.
Appropriate use	It is recommended that Romania take steps to ensure that the appropriate use condition is met.

The domestic legal and administrative framework

It is recommended that Romania take steps amend its legislation or otherwise clarify that local filing is only required in line with the minimum standard for Action 13. This recommendation remains in place since the 2017/2018 review.

The exchange of information framework

It is recommended that Romania take steps to implement processes or written procedures to ensure that the exchange of information is conducted in a manner consistent with the terms of reference relating to the exchange of information framework. This recommendation remains in place since the 2018/2019 peer review.

Romania made some exchanges of CbC reports after the deadline. This was caused by a technical issue, which has since been resolved and so no recommendation is required.

Appropriate use of CbC reports

Romania does not yet have controls in place to ensure the appropriate use of CbC reports.

It is recommended that Romania take steps to ensure that the appropriate use condition is met. This recommendation remains in place since the 2017/2018 peer review.

Russian Federation

Overview of CbC reporting requirements

First reporting fiscal year: Commencing on or after 1 January 2017

Consolidated group revenue threshold: RUB 50 billion

Filing deadline: 12 months following the end of the reporting fiscal year

Local filing required: Yes

Surrogate parent entity filing permitted: Yes

First review of the domestic legal framework: 2017/2018

Summary of recommendations

Area of implementation	Recommendations for improvement
Domestic legal and administrative framework	It is recommended that Russia amend its legislation or otherwise takes steps to ensure that local filing is only required in the circumstances contained in the terms of reference. It is recommended that Russia amend its legislation or otherwise take steps to ensure that enforcement provisions and monitoring relating to CbC reporting's effective implementation are provided for as contained in the terms of reference as from the first reporting period.
Exchange of information framework	None.
Appropriate use	None.

The domestic legal and administrative framework

It is recommended that Russia amend its legislation or otherwise takes steps to ensure that local filing is only required in the circumstances contained in the terms of reference. This recommendation remains in place since the 2017/2018 peer review.

It is recommended that Russia amend its legislation or otherwise take steps to ensure that enforcement provisions and monitoring relating to CbC reporting's effective implementation are provided for as contained in the terms of reference as from the first reporting period. This recommendation remains in place since the 2017/2018 peer review.

The exchange of information framework

Russia confirms that its rules have not changed and continue to be applied effectively. Russia continues to meet all terms of reference.

Appropriate use of CbC reports

Russia confirms that its rules have not changed and continue to be applied effectively. Russia continues to meet all terms of reference.

Saint Lucia

Overview of CbC reporting requirements

Saint Lucia has not yet introduced a requirement for the filing of CbC reports, as required under the BEPS Action 13 (CbC reporting) minimum standard.

Summary of recommendations

Area of implementation	Recommendations for improvement
Domestic legal and administrative framework	It is recommended that Saint Lucia take steps to implement a domestic legal and administrative framework to impose and enforce CbC reporting requirements as soon as possible.
Exchange of information framework	It is recommended that Saint Lucia take steps to have qualifying competent authority agreements in effect with jurisdictions of the Inclusive Framework that meet the confidentiality, consistency and appropriate use conditions and with which Saint Lucia has an international exchange of information agreement in effect that allows for the automatic exchange of tax information. It is recommended that Saint Lucia take steps to implement the necessary processes or written procedures to ensure that the exchange of information is conducted in a manner consistent with the terms of reference relating to the exchange of information framework.
Appropriate use	It is recommended that Saint Lucia take steps to ensure that the appropriate use condition is met ahead of the first exchanges of information.

The domestic legal and administrative framework

Saint Lucia does not yet have legislation in place to implement the BEPS Action 13 minimum standard.

It is recommended that Saint Lucia take steps to implement a domestic legal and administrative framework to impose and enforce CbC reporting requirements as soon as possible. This recommendation remains in place since the 2018/2019 peer review.

The exchange of information framework

Saint Lucia has no bilateral relationships in place for the exchange of CbC reports nor processes to ensure that the exchange of information is conducted in a manner consistent with the terms of reference relating to the exchange of information framework.

It is recommended that Saint Lucia take steps to have qualifying competent authority agreements in effect with jurisdictions of the Inclusive Framework that meet the confidentiality, consistency and appropriate use conditions and with which Saint Lucia has an international exchange of information agreement in effect that allows for the automatic exchange of tax information. This recommendation remains in place since the 2018/2019 peer review.

It is recommended that Saint Lucia take steps to implement the necessary processes or written procedures to ensure that the exchange of information is conducted in a manner consistent with the terms of reference relating to the exchange of information framework. This recommendation remains in place since the 2018/2019 peer review.

Appropriate use of CbC reports

Saint Lucia does not yet have controls in place to ensure the appropriate use of CbC reports.

It is recommended that Saint Lucia take steps to ensure that the appropriate use condition is met ahead of the first exchanges of information. This recommendation remains in place since the 2018/2019 peer review.

Saint Vincent and the Grenadines

Overview of CbC reporting requirements

Saint Vincent and the Grenadines has not yet introduced a requirement for the filing of CbC reports, as required under the BEPS Action 13 (CbC reporting) minimum standard.

Summary of recommendations

Area of implementation	Recommendations for improvement
Domestic legal and administrative framework	It is recommended that Saint Vincent and the Grenadines take steps to implement a domestic legal and administrative framework to impose and enforce CbC reporting requirements as soon as possible.
Exchange of information framework	It is recommended that Saint Vincent and the Grenadines take steps to have qualifying competent authority agreements in effect with jurisdictions of the Inclusive Framework that meet the confidentiality, consistency and appropriate use conditions and with which Saint Vincent and the Grenadines has an international exchange of information agreement in effect that allows for the automatic exchange of tax information. It is recommended that Saint Vincent and the Grenadines take steps to implement the necessary processes or written procedures to ensure that the exchange of information is conducted in a manner consistent with the terms of reference relating to the exchange of information framework.
Appropriate use	It is recommended that Saint Vincent and the Grenadines take steps to ensure that the appropriate use condition is met ahead of the first exchanges of information.

The domestic legal and administrative framework

Saint Vincent and the Grenadines does not yet have legislation in place to implement the BEPS Action 13 minimum standard.

It is recommended that Saint Vincent and the Grenadines take steps to implement a domestic legal and administrative framework to impose and enforce CbC reporting requirements as soon as possible. This recommendation remains in place since the 2019/2020 peer review.

The exchange of information framework

Saint Vincent and the Grenadines has no bilateral relationships in place for the exchange of CbC reports nor processes to ensure that the exchange of information is conducted in a manner consistent with the terms of reference relating to the exchange of information framework.

It is recommended that Saint Vincent and the Grenadines take steps to have qualifying competent authority agreements in effect with jurisdictions of the Inclusive Framework that meet the confidentiality, consistency and appropriate use conditions and with which Saint Vincent and the Grenadines has an international exchange of information agreement in effect that allows for the automatic exchange of tax information. This recommendation remains in place since the 2019/2020 peer review.

It is recommended that Saint Vincent and the Grenadines take steps to implement the necessary processes or written procedures to ensure that the exchange of information is conducted in a manner consistent with the terms of reference relating to the exchange of information framework. This recommendation remains in place since the 2019/2020 peer review.

Appropriate use of CbC reports

Saint Vincent and the Grenadines does not yet have controls in place to ensure the appropriate use of CbC reports.

It is recommended that Saint Vincent and the Grenadines take steps to ensure that the appropriate use condition is met ahead of the first exchanges of information. This recommendation remains in place since the 2019/2020 peer review.

San Marino

Overview of CbC reporting requirements

First reporting fiscal year: Commencing on or after 1 January 2019

Consolidated group revenue threshold: EUR 750 million

Filing deadline: 12 months following the end of the reporting fiscal year

Local filing required: Yes

Surrogate parent entity filing permitted: Yes

First review of the domestic legal framework: 2018/2019

Summary of recommendations

Area of implementation	Recommendations for improvement
Domestic legal and administrative framework	None.
Exchange of information framework	None.
Appropriate use	None.

The domestic legal and administrative framework

San Marino confirms that its rules have not changed and continue to be applied effectively. San Marino continues to meet all terms of reference.

The exchange of information framework

San Marino confirms that its rules have not changed and continue to be applied effectively. San Marino continues to meet all terms of reference.

Appropriate use of CbC reports

San Marino confirms that its rules have not changed and continue to be applied effectively. San Marino continues to meet all terms of reference.

Saudi Arabia

Overview of CbC reporting requirements

First reporting fiscal year: Commencing on or after 1 January 2018

Consolidated group revenue threshold: SAR 3.2 billion

Filing deadline: 12 months following the end of the reporting fiscal year

Local filing required: Yes

Surrogate parent entity filing permitted: Yes

First review of the domestic legal framework: 2019/2020

Summary of recommendations

Area of implementation	Recommendations for improvement
Domestic legal and administrative framework	None.
Exchange of information framework	None.
Appropriate use	None.

The domestic legal and administrative framework

Saudi Arabia confirms that its rules have not changed and continue to be applied effectively. Saudi Arabia continues to meet all terms of reference

The exchange of information framework

Saudi Arabia confirms that its rules have not changed and continue to be applied effectively. Saudi Arabia continues to meet all terms of reference.

Appropriate use of CbC reports

Saudi Arabia confirms that its rules have not changed and continue to be applied effectively. Saudi Arabia continues to meet all terms of reference.

Senegal

Overview of CbC reporting requirements

First reporting fiscal year: Commencing on or after 1 January 2018

Consolidated group revenue threshold: XOF 49,967,750,000

Filing deadline: 12 months following the end of the reporting fiscal year

Local filing required: Yes

Surrogate parent entity filing permitted: Yes

First review of the domestic legal framework: 2018/2019

Summary of recommendations

Area of implementation	Recommendations for improvement
Domestic legal and administrative framework	It is recommended that Senegal finalise its domestic legal and administrative framework as soon as possible. Specifically, it is recommended that Senegal: • introduce or complete the definitions of an "Ultimate Parent Entity", "MNE Group", "Group" and "Constituent Entity" in a manner that is consistent with the terms of reference; • publish the content and format of a CbC report; • amend or otherwise clarify the annual consolidated revenue threshold calculation rule in respect of MNE Groups whose Ultimate Parent Entity is located in a jurisdiction other than Senegal which may deviate from the guidance issued by the OECD; • amend the conditions for local filing or otherwise take steps to ensure that local filing can only be required in the circumstances permitted under the minimum standard; • have enforcement measures in place in case of incomplete or erroneous filing.
Exchange of information framework	It is recommended that Senegal take steps to have qualifying competent authority agreements in effect with jurisdictions of the Inclusive Framework which meet the confidentiality, consistency and appropriate use conditions and with which Senegal has an international exchange of information agreement in effect that allows for the automatic exchange of tax information. It is recommended that Senegal have in place the necessary processes or written procedures to ensure that the exchange of information is conducted in a manner consistent with the terms of reference relating to the exchange of information framework.
Appropriate use	It is recommended that Senegal take steps to ensure that the appropriate use condition is met ahead of the first exchanges of information.

The domestic legal and administrative framework

It is recommended that Senegal finalise its domestic legal and administrative framework as soon as possible. Specifically, it is recommended that Senegal:

- introduce or complete the definitions of an "Ultimate Parent Entity", "MNE Group", "Group" and "Constituent Entity" in a manner that is consistent with the terms of reference;
- publish the content and format of a CbC report;
- amend or otherwise clarify the annual consolidated revenue threshold calculation rule in respect of MNE Groups whose Ultimate Parent Entity is located in a jurisdiction other than Senegal which may deviate from the guidance issued by the OECD;
- amend the conditions for local filing or otherwise take steps to ensure that local filing can only be required in the circumstances permitted under the minimum standard;

- have enforcement measures in place in case of incomplete or erroneous filing.

These recommendations remain in place since the 2017/2018 peer report.[1] [2]

The exchange of information framework

Senegal has no bilateral relationships in place for the exchange of CbC reports nor processes to ensure that the exchange of information is conducted in a manner consistent with the terms of reference relating to the exchange of information framework.

It is recommended that Senegal take steps to have qualifying competent authority agreements in effect with jurisdictions of the Inclusive Framework which meet the confidentiality, consistency and appropriate use conditions and with which Senegal has an international exchange of information agreement in effect that allows for the automatic exchange of tax information. This recommendation remains in place since the 2017/2018 peer review.

It is recommended that Senegal have in place the necessary processes or written procedures to ensure that the exchange of information is conducted in a manner consistent with the terms of reference relating to the exchange of information framework. This recommendation remains in place since the 2017/2018 peer review.

Appropriate use of CbC reports

Senegal does not yet have controls in place to ensure the appropriate use of CbC reports.

It is recommended that Senegal take steps to ensure that the appropriate use condition is met ahead of the first exchanges of information. This recommendation remains in place since the 2017/2018 peer review.

Notes

[1] Senegal's local filing requirements will not apply if there is surrogate filing in another jurisdiction which is listed in a list of states or territories which have adopted regulations imposing the filing of a CbC report similar to that required in Senegal, which have concluded an agreement with Senegal for the automatic exchange of CbC reports and which comply with the obligations arising from such agreement. It is unclear whether local filing would be "deactivated" in respect of jurisdictions which allow voluntary parent surrogate filing, being noted that the list mentioned above has not yet been published at this point in time. A monitoring point on this remains in place since the 2018/2019 peer review.

[2] There are no specific processes in place that would allow Senegal to take appropriate measures in case it is notified by another jurisdiction that such other jurisdiction has reason to believe that an error may have led to incorrect or incomplete information reporting by a Reporting Entity or that there is non-compliance of a Reporting Entity with respect to its obligation to file a CbC report. As no exchange of CbC reports has yet occurred, this aspect is being monitored. This monitoring point remains in place since the 2018/2019 peer review.

Serbia

Overview of CbC reporting requirements

First reporting fiscal year: Commencing on or after 1 January 2020

Consolidated group revenue threshold: EUR 750 million

Filing deadline: 12 months following the end of the reporting fiscal year

Local filing required: No

Surrogate parent entity filing permitted: No

First review of the domestic legal framework: 2020/2021

Summary of recommendations

Area of implementation	Recommendations for improvement
Domestic legal and administrative framework	None.
Exchange of information framework	It is recommended that Serbia take steps to have qualifying competent authority agreements in effect with jurisdictions of the Inclusive Framework that meet the confidentiality, consistency and appropriate use conditions and with which Serbia has an international exchange of information agreement in effect that allows for the automatic exchange of tax information. It is recommended that Serbia take steps to implement the necessary processes or written procedures to ensure that the exchange of information is conducted in a manner consistent with the terms of reference relating to the exchange of information framework.
Appropriate use	It is recommended that Serbia take steps to ensure that the appropriate use condition is met ahead of the first exchanges of information.

The domestic legal and administrative framework

Serbia's 2020/2021 review recommended that Serbia take steps to implement legislation or guidance to set out the requirements as to the form and content of a CbC report. This guidance has now been published and the recommendation is therefore removed.

Serbia's domestic legal and administrative framework meets all other terms of reference.

The exchange of information framework

Serbia has no bilateral relationships in place for the exchange of CbC reports nor processes to ensure that the exchange of information is conducted in a manner consistent with the terms of reference relating to the exchange of information framework.

It is recommended that Serbia take steps to have qualifying competent authority agreements in effect with jurisdictions of the Inclusive Framework that meet the confidentiality, consistency and appropriate use conditions and with which Serbia has an international exchange of information agreement in effect that allows for the automatic exchange of tax information. This recommendation remains in place since the 2018/2019 peer review.

It is recommended that Serbia take steps to implement the necessary processes or written procedures to ensure that the exchange of information is conducted in a manner consistent with the terms of reference relating to the exchange of information framework. This recommendation remains in place since the 2018/2019 peer review.

Appropriate use of CbC reports

Serbia does not yet have controls in place to ensure the appropriate use of CbC reports.

It is recommended that Serbia take steps to ensure that the appropriate use condition is met ahead of the first exchanges of information. This recommendation remains in place since the 2018/2019 peer review.

Seychelles

Overview of CbC reporting requirements

First reporting fiscal year: Commencing on or after 1 January 2018.

Consolidated group revenue threshold: EUR 750 million

Filing deadline: 12 months following the end of the reporting fiscal year

Local filing required: No

Surrogate parent entity filing permitted: No

First review of the domestic legal framework: 2017/2018

Summary of recommendations

Area of implementation	Recommendations for improvement
Domestic legal and administrative framework	None
Exchange of information framework	It is recommended that the Seychelles take steps to implement processes or written procedures to ensure that the exchange of information is conducted in a manner consistent with the terms of reference relating to the exchange of information framework as soon as possible.
Appropriate use	It is recommended that the Seychelles take steps to ensure that the appropriate use condition is met as soon as possible.

The domestic legal and administrative framework

Seychelles confirms that its rules have not changed and continue to be applied effectively. Seychelles continues to meet all terms of reference.

The exchange of information framework

It is recommended that the Seychelles take steps to implement processes or written procedures to ensure that the exchange of information is conducted in a manner consistent with the terms of reference relating to the exchange of information framework as soon as possible. This recommendation remains in place since the 2018/2019 peer review.

Appropriate use of CbC reports

Seychelles does not yet have controls in place to ensure the appropriate use of CbC reports.

It is recommended that the Seychelles take steps to ensure that the appropriate use condition is met as soon as possible. This recommendation remains in place since the 2017/2018 peer review.

Sierra Leone

Overview of CbC reporting requirements

Sierra Leone has not yet introduced a requirement for the filing of CbC reports, as required under the BEPS Action 13 (CbC reporting) minimum standard.

Summary of recommendations

Area of implementation	Recommendations for improvement
Domestic legal and administrative framework	It is recommended that Sierra Leone take steps to implement a domestic legal and administrative framework to impose and enforce CbC reporting requirements as soon as possible.
Exchange of information framework	It is recommended that Sierra Leone take steps to have qualifying competent authority agreements in effect with jurisdictions of the Inclusive Framework that meet the confidentiality, consistency and appropriate use conditions and with which Sierra Leone has an international exchange of information agreement in effect that allows for the automatic exchange of tax information. It is recommended that Sierra Leone take steps to implement the necessary processes or written procedures to ensure that the exchange of information is conducted in a manner consistent with the terms of reference relating to the exchange of information framework.
Appropriate use	It is recommended that Sierra Leone take steps to ensure that the appropriate use condition is met ahead of the first exchanges of information.

The domestic legal and administrative framework

Sierra Leone does not yet have legislation in place to implement the BEPS Action 13 minimum standard.

It is recommended that Sierra Leone take steps to implement a domestic legal and administrative framework to impose and enforce CbC reporting requirements as soon as possible. This recommendation remains in place since the 2018/2019 peer review.

The exchange of information framework

Sierra Leone has no bilateral relationships in place for the exchange of CbC reports nor processes to ensure that the exchange of information is conducted in a manner consistent with the terms of reference relating to the exchange of information framework.

It is recommended that Sierra Leone take steps to have qualifying competent authority agreements in effect with jurisdictions of the Inclusive Framework that meet the confidentiality, consistency and appropriate use conditions and with which Sierra Leone has an international exchange of information agreement in effect that allows for the automatic exchange of tax information. This recommendation remains in place since the 2018/2019 peer review.

It is recommended that Sierra Leone take steps to implement the necessary processes or written procedures to ensure that the exchange of information is conducted in a manner consistent with the terms of reference relating to the exchange of information framework. This recommendation remains in place since the 2018/2019 peer review.

Appropriate use of CbC reports

Sierra Leone does not yet have controls in place to ensure the appropriate use of CbC reports.

It is recommended that Sierra Leone take steps to ensure that the appropriate use condition is met ahead of the first exchanges of information. This recommendation remains in place since the 2018/2019 peer review.

Singapore

Overview of CbC reporting requirements

First reporting fiscal year: Commencing on or after 1 January 2017. Singapore also allowed MNE Groups to file a CbC report on a voluntary basis, for reporting fiscal years commencing between 1 January 2016 and 31 December 2016.

Consolidated group revenue threshold: SGD 1.125 billion

Filing deadline: 12 months following the end of the reporting fiscal year

Local filing required: No

Surrogate parent entity filing permitted: Yes

First review of the domestic legal framework: 2017/2018

Summary of recommendations

Area of implementation	Recommendations for improvement
Domestic legal and administrative framework	None.
Exchange of information framework	None.
Appropriate use	None.

The domestic legal and administrative framework

Singapore confirms that its rules have not changed and continue to be applied effectively.[1] Singapore continues to meet all terms of reference.[2] [3] [4] [5]

The exchange of information framework

Singapore confirms that its rules have not changed and continue to be applied effectively. Singapore continues to meet all terms of reference.

Appropriate use of CbC reports

Singapore confirms that its rules have not changed and continue to be applied effectively. Singapore continues to meet all terms of reference.

Notes

[1] Singapore has clarified that the Convention on Mutual Administrative Assistance in Tax Matters has been incorporated in the domestic tax law and entered into force on 1 May 2016.

[2] Singapore's 2017/2018 peer review included a monitoring point in relation to a "designation provision". This monitoring point remains in place.

[3] Singapore's 2017/2018 peer review included a monitoring point in relation to the ability of the Comptroller to allow a CbC report to be filed later than the filing deadline as set in the regulations. This monitoring point remains in place.

[4] Singapore's 2017/2018 peer review included a monitoring point whereby if local filing requirements were introduced, these requirements should comply with the terms of reference under paragraph 8 (c). This monitoring point remains in place.

[5] Singapore's 2017/2018 peer review included a monitoring point whereby if local filing requirements were introduced, these requirements should be deactivated in case of surrogate filing in a manner consistent with the terms of reference under paragraph 8 (d). This monitoring point remains in place.

Slovak Republic

Overview of CbC reporting requirements

First reporting fiscal year: Commencing on or after 1 January 2016

Consolidated group revenue threshold: EUR 750 million

Filing deadline: 12 months following the end of the reporting fiscal year

Local filing required: Yes, for reporting fiscal years commencing on or after 1 January 2017

Surrogate parent entity filing permitted: Yes

First review of the domestic legal framework: 2017/2018

Summary of recommendations

Area of implementation	Recommendations for improvement
Domestic legal and administrative framework	None.
Exchange of information framework	None.
Appropriate use	None.

The domestic legal and administrative framework

The Slovak Republic confirms that its rules have not changed and continue to be applied effectively. The Slovak Republic continues to meet all terms of reference.

The exchange of information framework

The Slovak Republic confirms that its rules have not changed and continue to be applied effectively. The Slovak Republic continues to meet all terms of reference.

Appropriate use of CbC reports

The Slovak Republic confirms that its rules have not changed and continue to be applied effectively. The Slovak Republic continues to meet all terms of reference.

Slovenia

Overview of CbC reporting requirements

First reporting fiscal year: Commencing on or after 1 January 2016

Consolidated group revenue threshold: EUR 750 million

Filing deadline: 12 months following the end of the reporting fiscal year

Local filing required: Yes, for reporting fiscal years commencing on or after 1 January 2017

Surrogate parent entity filing permitted: Yes

First review of the domestic legal framework: 2017/2018

Summary of recommendations

Area of implementation	Recommendations for improvement
Domestic legal and administrative framework	None.
Exchange of information framework	None.
Appropriate use	None.

The domestic legal and administrative framework

Slovenia confirms that its rules have not changed and continue to be applied effectively. Slovenia continues to meet all terms of reference.[1]

The exchange of information framework

Slovenia confirms that its rules have not changed and continue to be applied effectively. Slovenia continues to meet all terms of reference.

Appropriate use of CbC reports

Slovenia confirms that its rules have not changed and continue to be applied effectively. Slovenia continues to meet all terms of reference.

Note

[1] Slovenia's 2017/2018 peer review included a general monitoring point relating to a specific process that would allow Slovenia to take appropriate measures in case Slovenia is notified by another jurisdiction that such other jurisdiction has reason to believe that an error may have led to incorrect or incomplete information reporting by a Reporting Entity or that there is non-compliance of a Reporting Entity with respect to its obligation to file a CbC report. This monitoring point remains in place.

South Africa

Overview of CbC reporting requirements

First reporting fiscal year: Commencing on or after 1 January 2016

Consolidated group revenue threshold: ZAR 10 billion

Filing deadline: 12 months following the end of the reporting fiscal year

Local filing required: Yes

Surrogate parent entity filing permitted: No

First review of the domestic legal framework: 2017/2018

Summary of recommendations

Area of implementation	Recommendations for improvement
Domestic legal and administrative framework	None.
Exchange of information framework	None.
Appropriate use	None.

The domestic legal and administrative framework

South Africa confirms that its rules have not changed and continue to be applied effectively. South Africa continues to meet all terms of reference.

The exchange of information framework

South Africa confirms that its rules have not changed and continue to be applied effectively. South Africa continues to meet all terms of reference.

Appropriate use of CbC reports

South Africa confirms that its rules have not changed and continue to be applied effectively. South Africa continues to meet all terms of reference.

Spain

Overview of CbC reporting requirements

First reporting fiscal year: Commencing on or after 1 January 2016

Consolidated group revenue threshold: EUR 750 million

Filing deadline: 12 months following the end of the reporting fiscal year

Local filing required: Yes

Surrogate parent entity filing permitted: Yes

First review of the domestic legal framework: 2017/2018

Summary of recommendations

Area of implementation	Recommendations for improvement
Domestic legal and administrative framework	It is recommended that Spain amend its legislation or otherwise clarify that the annual consolidated group revenue threshold calculation applies in a manner consistent with the OECD guidance on currency fluctuations in respect of an MNE Group whose Ultimate Parent Entity is located in a jurisdiction other than Spain, when local filing requirements are applicable. It is recommended that Spain amend its legislation or otherwise clarify the definition of a Constituent Entity to be included in a CbC report in a manner consistent with the terms of reference.
Exchange of information framework	None.
Appropriate use	None.

The domestic legal and administrative framework

It is recommended that Spain amend its legislation or otherwise clarify that the annual consolidated group revenue threshold calculation applies in a manner consistent with the OECD guidance on currency fluctuations in respect of an MNE Group whose Ultimate Parent Entity is located in a jurisdiction other than Spain, when local filing requirements are applicable. This recommendation remains in place since the 2017/2018 peer review.

It is recommended that Spain amend its legislation or otherwise clarify the definition of a Constituent Entity to be included in a CbC report in a manner consistent with the terms of reference. This recommendation remains in place since the 2017/2018 peer review.[1] [2]

The exchange of information framework

Spain confirms that its rules have not changed and continue to be applied effectively. Spain continues to meet all terms of reference.

Appropriate use of CbC reports

Spain confirms that its rules have not changed and continue to be applied effectively. Spain continues to meet all terms of reference.

Notes

[1] Spain's 2017/2018 peer review included a monitoring point on the potential exclusion of companies which are not required to produce consolidated financial statements from the filing requirement with respect to the absence in the definition of a "dominant company" of the "deemed listing provision". This monitoring point remains in place.

[2] Spain's 2017/2018 peer review included a monitoring point with respect to the absence of a provision relating to the "Source of data" to complete a CbC report. This monitoring point remains in place.

Sri Lanka

Overview of CbC reporting requirements

First reporting fiscal year: Commencing on or after 1 April 2018

Consolidated group revenue threshold: EUR 750 million or its equivalent in LKR

Filing deadline: 12 months following the end of the reporting fiscal year

Local filing required: Yes

Surrogate parent entity filing permitted: Yes

First review of the domestic legal framework: 2018/2019

Summary of recommendations

Area of implementation	Recommendations for improvement
Domestic legal and administrative framework	It is recommended that Sri Lanka amend or otherwise clarify the annual consolidated group revenue threshold calculation rule applies in a manner consistent with the OECD guidance on currency fluctuations in respect of an MNE Group whose Ultimate Parent entity is located in a jurisdiction other than Sri Lanka. It is recommended that Sri Lanka e take steps to ensure that local filing only occurs in the circumstances permitted under the minimum standard..
Exchange of information framework	It is recommended that Sri Lanka take steps to have qualifying competent authority agreements in effect with jurisdictions of the Inclusive Framework which meet the confidentiality, consistency and appropriate use conditions and with which it has an international exchange of information agreement in effect that allows for the automatic exchange of tax information. It is recommended that Sri Lanka take steps to implement the necessary processes or written procedures to ensure that the exchange of information is conducted in a manner consistent with the terms of reference relating to the exchange of information framework.
Appropriate use	It is recommended that Sri Lanka take steps to ensure that the appropriate use condition is met ahead of the first exchanges of information.

The domestic legal and administrative framework

It is recommended that Sri Lanka amend or otherwise clarify the annual consolidated group revenue threshold calculation rule applies in a manner consistent with the OECD guidance on currency fluctuations in respect of an MNE Group whose Ultimate Parent entity is located in a jurisdiction other than Sri Lanka. This recommendation remains in place since the 2018/2019 peer review.

It is recommended that Sri Lanka take steps to ensure that local filing only occurs in the circumstances permitted under the minimum standard. This recommendation remains in place since the 2018/2019 peer review.[1]

The exchange of information framework

Sri Lanka has no bilateral relationships in place for the exchange of CbC reports nor processes to ensure that the exchange of information is conducted in a manner consistent with the terms of reference relating to the exchange of information framework.

It is recommended that Sri Lanka take steps to have qualifying competent authority agreements in effect with jurisdictions of the Inclusive Framework which meet the confidentiality, consistency and appropriate use conditions and with which it has an international exchange of information agreement in effect that allows for the automatic exchange of tax information. This recommendation remains in place since the 2018/2019 peer review.

It is recommended that Sri Lanka take steps to implement the necessary processes or written procedures to ensure that the exchange of information is conducted in a manner consistent with the terms of reference relating to the exchange of information framework. This recommendation remains in place since the 2018/2019 peer review.

Appropriate use of CbC reports

Sri Lanka does not yet have controls in place to ensure the appropriate use of CbC reports.

It is recommended that Sri Lanka take steps to ensure that the appropriate use condition is met ahead of the first exchanges of information. This recommendation remains in place since the 2018/2019 peer review.

Note

[1] Sri Lanka's Regulations on Transfer Pricing refer to the responsibility to prepare and maintain transfer pricing documentation including the Country-by-Country Report applying to enterprises carrying out controlled transactions with associated enterprises subject to sections of Sri Lanka's primary legislation. This narrows the population of MNEs required to file a CbC report in Sri Lanka and apparently applies an exemption from reporting to MNEs who meet the threshold requirement but do not carry out controlled transactions with associated enterprises. In practice this is very unlikely to be the case for MNEs who would otherwise meet the requirement so no recommendation is made but the situation will be monitored. This monitoring point remains in place since the 2018/2019 peer review.

Sweden

Overview of CbC reporting requirements

First reporting fiscal year: Commencing on or after 1 January 2016

Consolidated group revenue threshold: SEK 7 billion

Filing deadline: 12 months following the end of the reporting fiscal year

Local filing required: Yes

Surrogate parent entity filing permitted: Yes

First review of the domestic legal framework: 2017/2018

Summary of recommendations

Area of implementation	Recommendations for improvement
Domestic legal and administrative framework	None.
Exchange of information framework	None.
Appropriate use	None.

The domestic legal and administrative framework

Sweden confirms that its rules have not changed and continue to be applied effectively. Sweden continues to meet all terms of reference.[1]

The exchange of information framework

Sweden confirms that its rules have not changed and continue to be applied effectively. Sweden continues to meet all terms of reference.

Appropriate use of CbC reports

Sweden confirms that its rules have not changed and continue to be applied effectively. Sweden continues to meet all terms of reference.

Note

[1] Sweden's 2017/2018 peer review included a monitoring point relating to the conditions under which local filing may be required (paragraph 8 (c) iv. b) of the terms of reference). This monitoring point remains in place.

Switzerland

Overview of CbC reporting requirements

First reporting fiscal year: Commencing on or after 1 January 2018. Switzerland also allowed MNE Groups to file a CbC report on a voluntary basis, for reporting fiscal years commencing between 1 January 2016 and 31 December 2017.

Consolidated group revenue threshold: CHF 900 million

Filing deadline: 12 months following the end of the reporting fiscal year

Local filing required: Yes

Surrogate parent entity filing permitted: Yes

First review of the domestic legal framework: 2017/2018

Summary of recommendations

Area of implementation	Recommendations for improvement
Domestic legal and administrative framework	None.
Exchange of information framework	None.
Appropriate use	None.

The domestic legal and administrative framework

Switzerland confirms that its rules have not changed and continue to be applied effectively. Switzerland continues to meet all terms of reference.

The exchange of information framework

Switzerland confirms that its rules have not changed and continue to be applied effectively. Switzerland continues to meet all terms of reference.

Appropriate use of CbC reports

Switzerland confirms that its rules have not changed and continue to be applied effectively. Switzerland continues to meet all terms of reference.

Thailand

Overview of CbC reporting requirements

First reporting fiscal year: Commencing on or after 1 January 2021

Consolidated group revenue threshold: THB 28,000,000,000

Filing deadline: 12 months following the end of the reporting fiscal year

Local filing required: Requirement suspended

Surrogate parent entity filing permitted: Yes

First review of the domestic legal framework: 2021/2022

Summary of recommendations

Area of implementation	Recommendations for improvement
Domestic legal and administrative framework	It is recommended that Thailand amend its legislation or otherwise take steps to ensure that enforcement provisions and monitoring relating to CbC reporting's effective implementation are provided for as contained in the terms of reference as from the first reporting period.
Exchange of information framework	It is recommended that Thailand take steps to have qualifying competent authority agreements in effect with jurisdictions of the Inclusive Framework that meet the confidentiality, consistency and appropriate use conditions and with which Thailand has an international exchange of information agreement in effect that allows for the automatic exchange of tax information. It is recommended that Thailand take steps to implement the necessary processes or written procedures to ensure that the exchange of information is conducted in a manner consistent with the terms of reference relating to the exchange of information framework.
Appropriate use	It is recommended that Thailand take steps to ensure that the appropriate use condition is met ahead of the first exchanges of information.

The domestic legal and administrative framework

In the 2017/2018 peer review, it was recommended that Thailand take steps to implement a domestic legal and administrative framework to impose and enforce CbC reporting requirements as soon as possible. Thailand has now introduced a CbC reporting filing requirement which applies to all Ultimate Parent Entities of MNE Groups above a certain threshold and which requires inclusion of all constituent entities. This recommendation is therefore removed.[1]

A CbC reporting filing obligation applies in Thailand for fiscal years commencing on or after 1 January 2021 and filing is required 12 months after the reporting year end.

Thailand has penalties in place in relation to the filing of a CbC report for failure to file and late filing. There are however, no penalties in relation to incomplete or erroneous filing of a CbC report. It is recommended that Thailand amend its legislation or otherwise take steps to ensure that enforcement provisions and monitoring relating to CbC reporting's effective implementation are provided for as contained in the terms of reference as from the first reporting period.

Thailand has a legislative requirement for local filing of CbC reports despite Thailand not meeting the requirements to allow for local filing. However, as the local filing requirement is currently suspended, no recommendation is required.[2]

Thailand's domestic legal and administrative framework meets all the other terms of reference.

The exchange of information framework

Thailand has no bilateral relationships in place for the exchange of CbC reports nor processes to ensure that the exchange of information is conducted in a manner consistent with the terms of reference relating to the exchange of information framework.

It is recommended that Thailand take steps to have qualifying competent authority agreements in effect with jurisdictions of the Inclusive Framework that meet the confidentiality, consistency and appropriate use conditions and with which Thailand has an international exchange of information agreement in effect that allows for the automatic exchange of tax information. This recommendation remains in place since the 2017/2018 peer review.

It is recommended that Thailand take steps to implement the necessary processes or written procedures to ensure that the exchange of information is conducted in a manner consistent with the terms of reference relating to the exchange of information framework. This recommendation remains in place since the 2018/2019 peer review.

Appropriate use of CbC reports

Thailand does not yet have controls in place to ensure the appropriate use of CbC reports.

It is recommended that Thailand take steps to ensure that the appropriate use condition is met ahead of the first exchanges of information. This recommendation remains in place since the 2017/2018 peer review.

Notes

[1] https://www.rd.go.th/fileadmin/user_upload/kormor/newlaw/dg408.pdf.

[2] https://cbcr.rd.go.th/aeoi/assets/Doc/cbcr_local_guidance.pdf.

Togo

Overview of CbC reporting requirements

Togo has not yet introduced a requirement for the filing of CbC reports, as required under the BEPS Action 13 (CbC reporting) minimum standard.

Summary of recommendations

Area of implementation	Recommendations for improvement
Domestic legal and administrative framework	It is recommended that Togo take steps to implement a domestic legal and administrative framework to impose and enforce CbC reporting requirements as soon as possible.
Exchange of information framework	It is recommended that Togo take steps to have qualifying competent authority agreements in effect with jurisdictions of the Inclusive Framework that meet the confidentiality, consistency and appropriate use conditions and with which Togo has an international exchange of information agreement in effect that allows for the automatic exchange of tax information. It is recommended that Togo take steps to implement the necessary processes or written procedures to ensure that the exchange of information is conducted in a manner consistent with the terms of reference relating to the exchange of information framework.
Appropriate use	It is recommended that Togo take steps to ensure that the appropriate use condition is met ahead of the first exchanges of information.

The domestic legal and administrative framework

Togo does not yet have legislation in place to implement the BEPS Action 13 minimum standard.

It is recommended that Togo take steps to implement a domestic legal and administrative framework to impose and enforce CbC reporting requirements as soon as possible.

The exchange of information framework

Togo has no bilateral relationships in place for the exchange of CbC reports nor processes to ensure that the exchange of information is conducted in a manner consistent with the terms of reference relating to the exchange of information framework.

It is recommended that Togo take steps to have qualifying competent authority agreements in effect with jurisdictions of the Inclusive Framework that meet the confidentiality, consistency and appropriate use conditions and with which Togo has an international exchange of information agreement in effect that allows for the automatic exchange of tax information.

It is recommended that Togo take steps to implement the necessary processes or written procedures to ensure that the exchange of information is conducted in a manner consistent with the terms of reference relating to the exchange of information framework.

Appropriate use of CbC reports

Togo does not yet have controls in place to ensure the appropriate use of CbC reports.

It is recommended that Togo take steps to ensure that the appropriate use condition is met ahead of the first exchanges of information.

Trinidad and Tobago

Overview of CbC reporting requirements

Trinidad and Tobago has not yet introduced a requirement for the filing of CbC reports, as required under the BEPS Action 13 (CbC reporting) minimum standard.

Summary of recommendations

Area of implementation	Recommendations for improvement
Domestic legal and administrative framework	It is recommended that Trinidad and Tobago take steps to implement a domestic legal and administrative framework to impose and enforce CbC reporting requirements as soon as possible.
Exchange of information framework	It is recommended that Trinidad and Tobago take steps to have qualifying competent authority agreements in effect with jurisdictions of the Inclusive Framework that meet the confidentiality, consistency and appropriate use conditions and with which Trinidad and Tobago has an international exchange of information agreement in effect that allows for the automatic exchange of tax information. It is recommended that Trinidad and Tobago take steps to implement the necessary processes or written procedures to ensure that the exchange of information is conducted in a manner consistent with the terms of reference relating to the exchange of information framework.
Appropriate use	It is recommended that Trinidad and Tobago take steps to ensure that the appropriate use condition is met ahead of the first exchanges of information.

The domestic legal and administrative framework

Trinidad and Tobago does not yet have legislation in place to implement the BEPS Action 13 minimum standard.

It is recommended that Trinidad and Tobago take steps to implement a domestic legal and administrative framework to impose and enforce CbC reporting requirements as soon as possible. This recommendation remains in place since the 2018/2019 peer review.

The exchange of information framework

Trinidad and Tobago has no bilateral relationships in place for the exchange of CbC reports nor processes to ensure that the exchange of information is conducted in a manner consistent with the terms of reference relating to the exchange of information framework.

It is recommended that Trinidad and Tobago take steps to have qualifying competent authority agreements in effect with jurisdictions of the Inclusive Framework that meet the confidentiality, consistency and appropriate use conditions and with which Trinidad and Tobago has an international exchange of information agreement in effect that allows for the automatic exchange of tax information. This recommendation remains in place since the 2018/2019 peer review.

It is recommended that Trinidad and Tobago take steps to implement the necessary processes or written procedures to ensure that the exchange of information is conducted in a manner consistent with the terms of reference relating to the exchange of information framework. This recommendation remains in place since the 2018/2019 peer review.

Appropriate use of CbC reports

Trinidad and Tobago does not yet have controls in place to ensure the appropriate use of CbC reports.

It is recommended that Trinidad and Tobago take steps to ensure that the appropriate use condition is met ahead of the first exchanges of information. This recommendation remains in place since the 2018/2019 peer review.

Tunisia

Overview of CbC reporting requirements

First reporting fiscal year: Commencing on or after 1 January 2020

Consolidated group revenue threshold: TND 1,636 million

Filing deadline: 12 months following the end of the reporting fiscal year

Local filing required: Requirement suspended

Surrogate parent entity filing permitted: Yes

First review of the domestic legal framework: 2018/2019

Summary of recommendations

Area of implementation	Recommendations for improvement
Domestic legal and administrative framework	None.
Exchange of information framework	It is recommended that Tunisia take steps to implement the necessary processes or written procedures to ensure that the exchange of information is conducted in a manner consistent with the terms of reference relating to the exchange of information framework.
Appropriate use	Not reviewed.

The domestic legal and administrative framework

The 2018/2019 peer review recommended that Tunisia introduce or complete the definitions of a " "Group", "MNE Group", "Constituent Entity", "Consolidated Financial Statements", "Fiscal Year", "Reporting Fiscal Year", "Qualifying Competent Authority Agreement" and "International Agreement" in a manner that is consistent with the terms of reference. These definitions have been amended and the recommendation is therefore removed.[1]

The 2018/2019 peer review recommended that Tunisia take steps to ensure that the annual consolidated group revenue threshold calculation rule is applied in a manner consistent with the OECD guidance on currency fluctuations. Tunisia has since amended its legislation to reflect this change and this recommendation is therefore removed.[2]

The 2018/2019 peer review recommended that Tunisia amend the conditions for local filing or otherwise take steps to ensure that local filing can only be required in the circumstances contained in the terms of reference. Tunisia has suspended its local filing requirement currently and this recommendation is removed.[3]

The 2018/2019 peer review recommended that Tunisia implement a provision whereby a single Constituent Entity of the same MNE Group may be designated to file the CbC report which would satisfy the local filing requirement of all the Constituent Entities in Tunisia. Tunisia has since amended its legislation to reflect this change and this recommendation is therefore removed.[4] [5]

Tunisia's domestic legal and administrative framework meets all other terms of reference.

The exchange of information framework

Tunisia's 2018/2019 peer review included a recommendation that Tunisia take steps to have qualifying competent authority agreements in effect with jurisdictions of the Inclusive Framework which meet the confidentiality, consistency and appropriate use conditions and with which Tunisia has an international exchange of information agreement in effect that allows for the automatic exchange of tax information. Tunisia has now activated relationships under the Multilateral Competent Authority Agreement for exchanging CbC reports and this recommendation is removed.

It is recommended that Tunisia take steps to implement processes or written procedures to ensure that the exchange of information is conducted in a manner consistent with the terms of reference relating to the exchange of information framework ahead of its first exchanges of information. This recommendation remains in place since the 2018/2019 peer review.

Appropriate use of CbC reports

Tunisia's 2018/2019 peer report recommended that steps be taken to ensure that the appropriate use condition is met ahead of the first exchanges of information.

Tunisia has submitted a notification under the CbC Multilateral Competent Authority Agreement that it is a non-reciprocal jurisdiction for CbC reporting purposes. As a non-reciprocal jurisdiction, Tunisia will not receive CbC reports submitted to tax authorities in other jurisdictions, and will not apply local filing. It is therefore not necessary for this peer review evaluation to reach any conclusions with respect to compliance with the terms of reference on appropriate use and this recommendation is removed.

Notes

[1] https://doc-fiscale.finances.gov.tn/cimf-internet/page/document/fr/preview?path=/Notes%20communes/2022/Note%20Commune%20N%C2%B013.pdf.

[2] https://doc-fiscale.finances.gov.tn/cimf-internet/page/document/fr/preview?path=/Notes%20communes/2022/Note%20Commune%20N%C2%B013.pdf.

[3] https://doc-fiscale.finances.gov.tn/cimf-internet/page/document/ar/preview?path=/%D9%85%D8%B0%D9%83%D8%B1%D8%A7%D8%AA%20%D8%B9%D8%A7%D9%85%D8%A9/2022/Note%20Commne%20N%C2%B018.pdf.

[4] https://doc-fiscale.finances.gov.tn/cimf-internet/page/document/fr/preview?path=/Notes%20communes/2022/Note%20Commune%20N%C2%B013.pdf.

[5] There are no specific processes in place that would allow Tunisia to take appropriate measures in case of notification by another jurisdiction that such other jurisdiction has reason to believe that an error may have led to incorrect or incomplete information reporting by a Reporting Entity or that there is non-compliance of a Reporting Entity with respect to CbC reporting obligations. As no exchange of CbC reports has yet occurred, no recommendation is made but this aspect will be further monitored. This monitoring point remains in place from the 2018/2019 peer review.

Türkiye

Overview of CbC reporting requirements

First reporting fiscal year: Commencing on or after 1 January 2019

Consolidated group revenue threshold: EUR 750 million

Filing deadline: 12 months following the end of the reporting fiscal year

Local filing required: Yes

Surrogate parent entity filing permitted: Yes

First review of the domestic legal framework: 2019/2020

Summary of recommendations

Area of implementation	Recommendations for improvement
Domestic legal and administrative framework	None.
Exchange of information framework	It is recommended that Türkiye take steps to have the necessary processes and written procedures to ensure that the exchange of information is conducted in a manner consistent with the terms of reference relating to the exchange of information framework.
Appropriate use	None.

The domestic legal and administrative framework

Türkiye confirms that its rules have not changed and continue to be applied effectively.

The exchange of information framework

It is recommended that Türkiye take steps to have the necessary processes and written procedures to ensure that the exchange of information is conducted in a manner consistent with the terms of reference relating to the exchange of information framework. This recommendation remains in place since the 2018/2019 peer report.

Türkiye made some exchanges of CbC reports after the deadline. This was due to technical challenges arising as part of the first year of exchange. These issues have been resolved, and so no recommendation is required.

Appropriate use of CbC reports

Türkiye's 2017/2018 peer review contained a recommendation that Türkiye take steps to ensure that the appropriate use condition is met. Türkiye has provided information to describe how this condition is met and this recommendation is now removed.

Turks and Caicos Islands

Overview of CbC reporting requirements

First reporting fiscal year: Commencing on or after 1 January 2020

Consolidated group revenue threshold: USD 850 million

Filing deadline: 12 months following the end of the reporting fiscal year

Local filing required: No

Surrogate parent entity filing permitted: No

First review of the domestic legal framework: 2018/2019

Summary of recommendations

Area of implementation	Recommendations for improvement
Domestic legal and administrative framework	None.
Exchange of information framework	It is recommended that Turks and Caicos Islands take steps to implement processes or written procedures to ensure that the exchange of information is conducted in a manner consistent with the terms of reference relating to the exchange of information framework ahead of the first exchanges of information.
Appropriate use	Not reviewed.

The domestic legal and administrative framework

Turks and Caicos Islands confirms that its rules have not changed and continue to be applied effectively. Turks and Caicos Islands continues to meet all terms of reference.

The exchange of information framework

It is recommended that Turks and Caicos Islands take steps to implement processes or written procedures to ensure that the exchange of information is conducted in a manner consistent with the terms of reference relating to the exchange of information framework ahead of the first exchanges of information. This recommendation remain in place from the 2018/2019 review.

Appropriate use of CbC reports

Turks and Caicos Islands is a non-reciprocal jurisdiction and, as such, will not receive CbC reports submitted to tax authorities in other jurisdictions, and will not apply local filing. It is therefore not necessary for this peer review evaluation to reach any conclusions with respect to compliance with the terms of reference on appropriate use.

Ukraine

Overview of CbC reporting requirements

First reporting fiscal year: Ending on or after 1 January 2021

Consolidated group revenue threshold: EUR 750 million

Filing deadline: 12 months following the end of the reporting fiscal year

Local filing required: Yes

Surrogate parent entity filing permitted: Yes

First review of the domestic legal framework: 2020/2021

Summary of recommendations

Area of implementation	Recommendations for improvement
Domestic legal and administrative framework	It is recommended that Ukraine amend its legislation or otherwise take steps to ensure that the definition of MNE Group is in line with that required by the Action 13 standard. It is recommended that Ukraine take steps to ensure that local filing only occurs in the circumstances permitted under the minimum standard. It is recommended that Ukraine clarify that the annual consolidated group revenue threshold calculation rule applies in line with the OECD guidance on currency fluctuations in respect of an MNE Group whose Ultimate Parent Entity is located in a jurisdiction other than Ukraine.
Exchange of information framework	It is recommended that Ukraine take steps to have qualifying competent authority agreements in effect with jurisdictions of the Inclusive Framework that meet the confidentiality, consistency and appropriate use conditions and with which Ukraine has an international exchange of information agreement in effect that allows for the automatic exchange of tax information It is recommended that Ukraine take steps to implement the necessary processes or written procedures to ensure that the exchange of information is conducted in a manner consistent with the terms of reference relating to the exchange of information framework.
Appropriate use	It is recommended that Ukraine take steps to ensure that the appropriate use condition is met ahead of the first exchanges of information.

The domestic legal and administrative framework

It is recommended that Ukraine amend its legislation or otherwise take steps to ensure that the definition of MNE Group is in line with that required in the Action 13 standard. This recommendation remains in place since the 2020/2021 peer review.

It is recommended that Ukraine amend its legislation or otherwise takes steps to ensure that local filing is only required in the circumstances permitted under the minimum standard. This recommendation remains in place since the 2020/2021 peer review.

It is recommended that Ukraine clarify that the annual consolidated group revenue threshold calculation rule applies in line with the OECD guidance on currency fluctuations in respect of an MNE Group whose Ultimate Parent Entity is located in a jurisdiction other than Ukraine. This recommendation remains in place since the 2020/2021 peer review.

Ukraine's domestic legal and administrative framework meets all other terms of reference.

The exchange of information framework

Ukraine has no bilateral relationships in place for the exchange of CbC reports nor processes to ensure that the exchange of information is conducted in a manner consistent with the terms of reference relating to the exchange of information framework.

It is recommended that Ukraine take steps to have qualifying competent authority agreements in effect with jurisdictions of the Inclusive Framework that meet the confidentiality, consistency and appropriate use conditions and with which Ukraine has an international exchange of information agreement in effect that allows for the automatic exchange of tax information. This recommendation remains in place since the 2017/2018 peer review.

It is recommended that Ukraine take steps to implement the necessary processes or written procedures to ensure that the exchange of information is conducted in a manner consistent with the terms of reference relating to the exchange of information framework. This recommendation remains in place since the 2018/2019 peer review.

Appropriate use of CbC reports

Ukraine does not yet have controls in place to ensure the appropriate use of CbC reports.

It is recommended that Ukraine take steps to ensure that the appropriate use condition is met ahead of the first exchanges of information. This recommendation remains in place since the 2017/2018 peer review.

United Arab Emirates

Overview of CbC reporting requirements

First reporting fiscal year: Commencing on or after 1 January 2019

Consolidated group revenue threshold: AED 3,150 million

Filing deadline: 12 months following the end of the reporting fiscal year

Local filing required: No

Surrogate parent entity filing permitted: No

First review of the domestic legal framework: 2019/2020

Summary of recommendations

Area of implementation	Recommendations for improvement
Domestic legal and administrative framework	None.
Exchange of information framework	None.
Appropriate use	Not reviewed.

The domestic legal and administrative framework

UAE confirms that its rules have not changed and continue to be applied effectively. UAE continues to meet all terms of reference.

The exchange of information framework

UAE confirms that its rules have not changed and continue to be applied effectively. UAE continues to meet all terms of reference.

Appropriate use of CbC reports

UAE is a non-reciprocal jurisdiction and, as such, will not receive CbC reports submitted to tax authorities in other jurisdictions, and will not apply local filing. It is therefore not necessary for this peer review evaluation to reach any conclusions with respect to compliance with the terms of reference on appropriate use.

United Kingdom

Overview of CbC reporting requirements

First reporting fiscal year: Commencing on or after 1 January 2016

Consolidated group revenue threshold: EUR 750 million

Filing deadline: 12 months following the end of the reporting fiscal year

Local filing required: Yes

Surrogate parent entity filing permitted: Yes

First review of the domestic legal framework: 2017/2018

Summary of recommendations

Area of implementation	Recommendations for improvement
Domestic legal and administrative framework	None.
Exchange of information framework	None.
Appropriate use	None.

The domestic legal and administrative framework

The United Kingdom confirms that its rules have not changed and continue to be applied effectively. The United Kingdom continues to meet all terms of reference.[1]

The exchange of information framework

The United Kingdom made some exchanges of CbC reports after the deadline. This was caused by a technical fault which has since been corrected and so no recommendation is required.

The United Kingdom confirms that its rules have not changed and continue to be applied effectively. The United Kingdom continues to meet all terms of reference.

Appropriate use of CbC reports

The United Kingdom confirms that its rules have not changed and continue to be applied effectively. The United Kingdom continues to meet all terms of reference.

Note

[1] The United Kingdom's 2017/2018 peer review included monitoring points with respect to the conditions under which local filing may be required (paragraph 8 (c) iv. b) and c) of the terms of reference). These monitoring points remain in place.

United States

Overview of CbC reporting requirements

First reporting fiscal year: Commencing on or after 30 June 2016, The United States also allowed MNE Groups to file a CbC report on a voluntary basis, for reporting fiscal years commencing between 1 January 2016 and 30 June 2016.

Consolidated group revenue threshold: USD 850 million

Filing deadline: with the annual income tax return

Local filing required: No

Surrogate parent entity filing permitted: Yes

First review of the domestic legal framework: 2017/2018

Summary of recommendations

Area of implementation	Recommendations for improvement
Domestic legal and administrative framework	It is recommended that the United States ensure that the definitions of "revenue" for the purposes of applying the threshold and for completing Table 1 are consistent with the definition in the Action 13 minimum standard, as further clarified by OECD guidance.
Exchange of information framework	It is recommended that the United States' competent authority should continue to work actively towards signing bilateral competent authority arrangements with jurisdictions of the Inclusive Framework that meet the confidentiality, consistency and appropriate use conditions, and with which the United States has an agreement in effect that allows for the automatic exchange of information.
Appropriate use	None.

The domestic legal and administrative framework

It is recommended that the United States ensure that the definitions of "revenue" for the purposes of applying the threshold and for completing Table 1 are consistent with the definition in the Action 13 minimum standard, as further clarified by OECD guidance. This recommendation remains in place since the 2017/2018 peer review.[1]

The exchange of information framework

It is recommended that the United States' competent authority should continue to work actively towards signing bilateral competent authority arrangements with jurisdictions of the Inclusive Framework that meet the confidentiality, consistency and appropriate use conditions, and with which the United States has an agreement in effect that allows for the automatic exchange of information. This recommendation remains in place since the 2017/2018 peer review.

Appropriate use of CbC reports

The United States confirms that its rules have not changed and continue to be applied effectively. The United States continues to meet all terms of reference.

Note

[1] The United States operates a modified filing requirement for MNEs which qualify as state security contractors. In light of the United States' explanations and the limited number of MNE Groups that are likely to qualify for the specified national security contractor status, no recommendation is made, but use of modified reporting will be monitored. This monitoring point remains in place since the 2018/2019 peer review.

Uruguay

Overview of CbC reporting requirements

First reporting fiscal year: Commencing on or after 1 January 2017

Consolidated group revenue threshold: EUR 750 million

Filing deadline: 12 months following the end of the reporting fiscal year

Local filing required: Yes

Surrogate parent entity filing permitted: Yes

First review of the domestic legal framework: 2017/2018

Summary of recommendations

Area of implementation	Recommendations for improvement
Domestic legal and administrative framework	It is recommended that Uruguay amend the conditions for local filing or otherwise take steps to ensure that local filing can only be required in the circumstances permitted under the minimum standard.
Exchange of information framework	None.
Appropriate use	None.

The domestic legal and administrative framework

It is recommended that Uruguay amend the conditions for local filing or otherwise take steps to ensure that local filing can only be required in the circumstances permitted under the minimum standard. This recommendation remains in place since the 2017/2018 peer review.

Uruguay's 2017/2018 peer review included a monitoring point relating to the absence of processes in place to take appropriate measures in case Uruguay is notified by another jurisdiction that an error may have led to incorrect or incomplete information reporting by a Reporting Entity or that there is noncompliance of a Reporting Entity with respect to its obligation to file a CbC report. Uruguay has put the relevant processes in place and so this monitoring point is now removed.

The exchange of information framework

Uruguay confirms that its rules have not changed and continue to be applied effectively. Uruguay continues to meet all terms of reference.

Appropriate use of CbC reports

Uruguay confirms that its rules have not changed and continue to be applied effectively. Uruguay continues to meet all terms of reference.

Viet Nam

Overview of CbC reporting requirements

First reporting fiscal year: Commencing on or after 1 May 2017

Consolidated group revenue threshold: VND 18,000 billion

Filing deadline: On demand

Local filing required: Yes

Surrogate parent entity filing permitted: Yes

First review of the domestic legal framework: 2018/2019

Summary of recommendations

Area of implementation	Recommendations for improvement
Domestic legal and administrative framework	It is recommended that Viet Nam amend its legislation or otherwise take steps to ensure that enforcement provisions relating to the effective implementation of CbC reporting filing requirements are provided for as soon as possible.
Exchange of information framework	It is recommended that Viet Nam take steps to have qualifying competent authority agreements in effect with jurisdictions of the Inclusive Framework which meet the confidentiality, consistency and appropriate use conditions and with which it has an international exchange of information agreement in effect that allows for the automatic exchange of tax information. It is recommended that Viet Nam take steps to implement processes or written procedures to ensure that the exchange of information is conducted in a manner consistent with the terms of reference relating to the exchange of information framework as soon as possible.
Appropriate use	It is recommended that Viet Nam take steps to ensure that the appropriate use condition is met as soon as possible.

The domestic legal and administrative framework

It is recommended that Viet Nam amend its legislation or otherwise take steps to ensure that enforcement provisions relating to effective implementation of filing requirement for CbC reporting are provided for as required by the terms of reference as soon as possible. This recommendation remains in place since the 2018/2019 peer review.

The local filing requirement in Viet Nam appears to be triggered in circumstances of suspension of an exchange relationship or a failure to exchange reports, which is a lesser requirement than that of systemic failure (defined in the BEPS Action 13 minimum standard as suspension for reasons other than those in accordance with the terms of the agreement or otherwise persistent failure to automatically exchange reports). Viet Nam has confirmed its intention to apply local filing in line with the minimum standard and it may be that this difference is an issue of translation, therefore no recommendation is made, but this issue will be monitored.

The exchange of information framework

Viet Nam has no bilateral relationships in place for the exchange of CbC reports nor processes to ensure that the exchange of information is conducted in a manner consistent with the terms of reference relating to the exchange of information framework.

It is recommended that Viet Nam take steps to have qualifying competent authority agreements in effect with jurisdictions of the Inclusive Framework which meet the confidentiality, consistency and appropriate use conditions and with which it has an international exchange of information agreement in effect that allows for the automatic exchange of tax information. This recommendation remains in place since the 2018/2019 peer review.

It is recommended that Viet Nam take steps to implement processes or written procedures to ensure that the exchange of information is conducted in a manner consistent with the terms of reference relating to the exchange of information framework as soon as possible. This recommendation remains in place since the 2018/2019 peer review.

Appropriate use of CbC reports

Viet Nam does not yet have controls in place to ensure the appropriate use of CbC reports.

It is recommended that Viet Nam take steps to ensure that the appropriate use condition is met as soon as possible. This recommendation remains in place since the 2018/2019 peer review.

Zambia

Overview of CbC reporting requirements

First reporting fiscal year: Ending on 31 December 2021

Consolidated group revenue threshold: EUR 750 million

Filing deadline: 12 months following the end of the reporting fiscal year

Local filing required: Yes

Surrogate parent entity filing permitted: Yes

First review of domestic legal framework: 2021/2022

Summary of recommendations

Area of implementation	Recommendations for improvement
Domestic legal and administrative framework	It is recommended that Zambia amend the definition of MNE Group or otherwise clarify the definition to be in line with the standard. It is recommended that Zambia amend the definition of Ultimate Parent Entity or otherwise clarify the definition to be in line with the standard. It is recommended that Zambia take steps to ensure that local filing only occurs in the circumstances permitted under the minimum standard. It is recommended that Zambia amend the definition of surrogate filing or otherwise clarify the definition to be in line with the standard. It is recommended that Zambia clarify that the annual consolidated group revenue threshold calculation rule applies in line with the OECD guidance on currency fluctuations in respect of an MNE Group whose Ultimate Parent Entity is located in a jurisdiction other than Zambia. It is recommended that Zambia publish the full content and format requirements of the CbC Report.
Exchange of information framework	It is recommended that Zambia take steps to have qualifying competent authority agreements in effect with jurisdictions of the Inclusive Framework that meet the confidentiality, consistency and appropriate use conditions and with which Zambia has an international exchange of information agreement in effect that allows for the automatic exchange of tax information. It is recommended that Zambia take steps to implement the necessary processes or written procedures to ensure that the exchange of information is conducted in a manner consistent with the terms of reference relating to the exchange of information framework.
Appropriate use	It is recommended that Zambia take steps to ensure that the appropriate use condition is met ahead of the first exchanges of information.

The domestic legal and administrative framework

Zambia's 2018/2019 peer review confirmed that Zambia has a legislative filing requirement in effect, but did not include a review of that legislation. Zambia's legislation has now been reviewed.

A legislative filing requirement is in effect which applies to all Ultimate Parent Entities of MNE Groups above a certain threshold and which required inclusion of all constituent entities.[1]

A CbC reporting filing obligation applies in Zambia for fiscal years ending on or after 31 December 2021 and filing is required within 12 months after the reporting year end. Zambia has enforcement requirements to ensure compliance with rules on CbC reporting.

There are a number of areas where there are recommendations to improve the legislation.

The definition of MNE Group

The definition in Zambia's legislation says: "multi-national enterprise group" meaning a group of associated business entities established in two or more States that is not an excluded multi-national enterprise group and includes an enterprise that is resident for tax purposes in one State and is subject to tax with respect to the business carried out through a permanent establishment in another State.

The definition of MNE group is intended to include businesses which are subject to tax in different jurisdictions, by having entities which are tax resident in different jurisdictions, or through being taxable in a different jurisdiction through a permanent establishment. The legislative reference to businesses being established rather than being tax resident in different jurisdictions, plus the use of "AND including an entity taxed through a permanent establishment" could be read as only applying to groups that have business through permanent establishments, so describing a narrower group of MNEs than the standard intends. It is recommended that Zambia amend the definition of MNE Group or otherwise clarify the definition to be in line with the standard.

The definition of Ultimate Parent Entity

The definition in Zambia's legislation says: "the constituent entity directly or indirectly owns a sufficient interest in one or more of the constituent entities of the multi-national enterprise group and it is required to prepare consolidated financial statements under accounting principles generally applied…"

The intention of this definition is to describe the entity at the top of the group which is required to produce consolidated accounts because of the level of interest it owns in other entities in the group, directly or indirectly. The legislative definition has the word "and" where the model legislation has "such that" and so does not have the specification on level of interest and could be read to include any entity in the group which prepares consolidated accounts. It is recommended that Zambia amend the definition of Ultimate Parent Entity or otherwise clarify the definition to be in line with the standard.

The local filing provision

The local filing definition in Zambia's legislation applies to "A constituent entity which is not an ultimate parent entity of a multi-national enterprise group" and the legislative definition of multinational enterprise group does not specifically exclude groups which do not meet the threshold requirement. This can be read as requiring constituent entities of all multinational groups of any size to make a local filing if the conditions are met and is therefore too broad. It is recommended that Zambia amend the definition of MNE groups to specify that it does include excluded MNE groups, or to otherwise specify a threshold requirement for local filing.

Zambia has a legislative requirement for local filing which is in effect despite Zambia not yet meeting all of the consistency, confidentiality and appropriate use conditions. It is therefore recommended that Zambia take steps to ensure that local filing only occurs in the circumstances permitted under the minimum standard.

The surrogate filing provision

The provision in Zambia's legislation relating to surrogate filing includes the condition that "the State of tax residence of the surrogate parent entity notifies the Commissioner-General of a system failure." This is incorrect. The requirement is that the jurisdiction of tax residence of the Surrogate Parent Entity has not notified a Systemic Failure. As written the legislation does not meet the requirement to dis-apply a local filing requirement where there is surrogate filing, except where a systemic failure has occurred and this will be very rare. It is recommended that Zambia amend the definition or otherwise clarify the definition to be in line with the standard.

Currency Fluctuations

Where an MNE Group draws up, or would draw up, its Consolidated Financial Statements in a currency other than that specified by Zambia, the reference to Zambia's threshold has the effect as if it were a reference to the equivalent in that currency at the average exchange rate for the accounting period. While this provision would not create an issue for MNE Groups whose Ultimate Parent Entity is a tax resident in Zambia, it may be incompatible with the guidance on currency fluctuations for MNE Groups whose Ultimate Parent Entity is located in another jurisdiction, if local filing requirements were applied in respect of a Constituent Entity (which is a Zambian tax resident) of an MNE Group which does not reach the threshold as determined in the jurisdiction of the Ultimate Parent Entity of such a Group.

It is recommended that Zambia clarify that the annual consolidated group revenue threshold calculation rule applies in line with the OECD guidance on currency fluctuations in respect of an MNE Group whose Ultimate Parent Entity is located in a jurisdiction other than Zambia.

Contents of the Country-by-Country report

The information included in the legislative Annex does not include all of the template of the Country-by-Country report and does not include any details of what should be included under each heading in the report. It is recommended that Zambia publish the full content and format requirements of the CbC Report.

The exchange of information framework

Zambia has no bilateral relationships in place for the exchange of CbC reports nor processes to ensure that the exchange of information is conducted in a manner consistent with the terms of reference relating to the exchange of information framework.

It is recommended that Zambia take steps to have qualifying competent authority agreements in effect with jurisdictions of the Inclusive Framework that meet the confidentiality, consistency and appropriate use conditions and with which Zambia has an international exchange of information agreement in effect that allows for the automatic exchange of tax information. This recommendation remains in place since the 2018/2019 peer review.

It is recommended that Zambia take steps to implement the necessary processes or written procedures to ensure that the exchange of information is conducted in a manner consistent with the terms of reference relating to the exchange of information framework. This recommendation remains in place since the 2018/2019 peer review.

Appropriate use of CbC reports

Zambia does not yet have controls in place to ensure the appropriate use of CbC reports.

It is recommended that Zambia take steps to ensure that the appropriate use condition is met ahead of the first exchanges of information. This recommendation remains in place since the 2018/2019 peer review.

Note

[1] https://www.enotices.co.zm/download/statutory-instrument-no-117-of-2020-the-income-tax-transfer-pricing-amendment-regulations-2020-pdf/.

9 789264 892132

Printed by Libri Plureos GmbH in Hamburg,
Germany